Map of the North & Centre of France

showing the chief places mentioned in the text

John Grandin

10 0 10 20 30

ILLE

Valenciennes

ouai

Cambrai

Guise

Laon
C E
iegne N
Vailly
ssons
Braisne

REIMS

Charleville
Mézières Sedan
Donchery

Rethel

Vouziers

Conflans
Gravelotte METZ

Verdun

Epernay

ux

Chalons
sur Marne

Bar-le-Duc

NANCY

Robert Sézanne

Ligny
en Barrois

STRASSBURG
Geispolsheim

Provins

Obernai

leau

Barr

Seine

Selestat

Sens

Meurthe

Turkheim Colmar
Gérardmer Neut
Ruffach Brisach
Guebwiller

Joigny

Tonnere Tanlay
Chablis Ancy le Franc

Thann

MULHOUSE

Auxerre

Avallon Epoisses
Semur

Belfort

Vezelay

Saone

Saulieu

DIJON
Chambertin

Nuits

BESANÇON

Doubs

Nevers

Pommard Beaune
Autun Meursault

Salins
Arbois
Champagnole

Chalons
sur Saone

St. Laurent

Morez

THE LAND OF FRANCE

1 Summer at the *Plage* *From the Water Colour by*
James McNeill Whistler

THE
LAND OF FRANCE

By

RALPH DUTTON

and

LORD HOLDEN

Illustrated from Photographs

NEW YORK

CHARLES SCRIBNER'S SONS

LONDON : B. T. BATSFORD LTD

1939

MADE AND PRINTED IN GREAT BRITAIN
BY WILLIAM CLOWES AND SONS, LIMITED
LONDON AND BECCLES

To

JOHN KARSLAKE

ACKNOWLEDGMENT

THE PUBLISHERS are particularly indebted to Mrs. Ruth Matthews and Mr. L. A. Audrain, by whom the majority of the photographs in this book were collected. They must also acknowledge their obligation to the photographers themselves, namely: J. Arnold, Colmar, for fig. 43; Brassai (Black Star), for figs. 55, 64, 65, 72, 124 and 132; la Cathédrale, Comminges, for fig. 108; Pierre Dubure, for figs. 93 and 107; Mr. Ralph Dutton, for figs. 4, 12, 15, 16, 32, 37, 39, 82, 91, 106, 119 and 122; Messrs. Fox Photos, Ltd., for fig. 7; Mr. Ewing Galloway (General Press Agency), for figs. 44, 61 and 96; Marcel Gautherot (Paul Popper), for fig. 40 ; Paul Kowaliski, for fig. 97; Lamballe (Black Star), for figs. 14 and 117; Ergy Landau (Black Star), for fig. 48; Messrs. Dorien Leigh, Ltd., for figs. 9, 10, 35, 54 and 110; Lévy et Neurdein, for fig. 17; Mr. F. S. Lincoln (Paul Popper), for figs. 6, 18, 29 and 33; Marcel Arthaud, for figs. 38 and 133; Matthieu, for fig. 70; René Messager (Black Star), for fig. 23; Mr. Lucien Myers, for figs. 13 and 100; Mr. Paul Popper, for figs. 88 and 89; Jean Roubier, for figs. 11, 24, 26, 28, 34, 36, 41, 43, 46, 47, 50, 52, 53, 57, 69, 73, 74, 75, 78, 79, 80, 83, 95, 98, 99, 101, 102, 104, 105, 111, 113, 114, 115, 116 and 130; Photo. Schall, for figs. 2, 3, 8, 19, 20, 21, 22, 25, 27, 30, 31, 42, 49, 50, 51, 56, 58, 59, 60, 62, 63, 66, 67, 68, 71, 76, 77, 81, 84, 85, 86, 87, 90, 92, 103, 118, 120, 121, 123, 125, 126, 127, 128, 129 and 131; Sélection, for fig. 94; Mr. Edward Wadsworth, for fig. 5; Messrs. Wide World Photos, for fig. 112; and Photo. Yvon, for fig. 109. The map-endpapers have been specially drawn for the book by Miss Norah Davenport.

CONTENTS

CHAPTER I

INTRODUCTION

THE great country of France covers approximately 210,000 square miles, about one-eighteenth of the total area of Europe or, if this should make the point any clearer, a space rather more than four times the size of England. It may seem rather presumptuous, when dealing with a country of this size, to attempt a description of the whole in a book of very moderate length; the authors therefore hasten, in introducing their work, to follow the advice of Robert Louis Stevenson : to "represent a delicate shade of manner between humility and superiority." They would first excuse themselves for endeavouring to dismiss in some 70,000 words a country which deserves a book of at least ten times that length, but at the same time would declare that they feel little contrition regarding the innumerable towns and places which have unavoidably been omitted from their pages.

The selection of subjects which have been chosen for inclusion may appear rather arbitrary at first sight, but there is in fact an underlying principle. We have endeavoured to give a general indication of the character of the different districts by describing the towns or countrysides which seem to us most typical of them, and which seem best to convey to a reader their particular "atmosphere." At the same time, we have where possible concentrated rather on lesser-known places than on the world-famous tourist centres. This has led to many glaring omissions; Avignon, for example, is passed by with barely a wave of the hand for the same reason that the Côte d'Azur is neglected: namely, that they are both so well known that they require no further praise to put them in the path of every tourist.

France, in our opinion, is unquestionably the finest touring country in the world, whether travel is by car, train, bicycle, or on foot. Nowhere else is there to be found such a happy union of a lovely countryside, studded with architectural and artistic beauties, with the material benefits of good food and wine and comfortable hotels in which to stay. Finally, it is at the present time extraordinarily cheap. The excitement of setting off by car from one of the French ports with the whole of France before one never dulls with repetition. There comes an increase in confidence, a lessening of anxiety regarding the difficulties

I   I

3 (*opposite*)
Poplars beside a Stream in the Orne

of the rule of the road, but the thrill and pleasure remain undimmed. After the crowded roads of England, it seems incredibly restful to cruise along the straight, well-surfaced avenues with seldom a car in sight, while the knowledge that an unfatiguing drive will bring one to a town with perhaps a cathedral or museum worth seeing, and almost certainly a lunch worth eating, is always sustaining.

There is one almost essential companion to a tour in France, the *Guide Michelin*, probably the best and most comprehensive guidebook in the world. It contains much information useful for cursory sight-seeing, but it is primarily a record of places in which to eat and sleep. In the information it gives on these subjects it is very rarely at fault. Consulting the *Michelin* adds zest and interest to every tour; the burning question will perpetually arise as to whether the pursuit of a restaurant with one more star merits an extra twenty miles on the road and a late arrival for lunch. The pages of this stout, narrow book rustle luxuriously as one turns them to scan the various possibilities and assess the merits of hotels and restaurants, while the clear, well-printed plans guide the driver through large and complicated towns with remarkable ease. Inevitably there are occasional disappoint-ments, though these are sometimes due to a change of owner-ship; but it more often happens that one finds an excellent meal in a place for which the *Guide* has shown no more than a modest enthusiasm.

There is a good excuse for being greedy in France, since the strong, clear air is in itself a stimulus to the appetite. Over the greater part of the country the climate is extremely bracing, and the majority of travellers feel an immediate access of vigour as soon as the Channel is crossed; the air may in general hardly deserve the well-worn epithet "Champagne," but it may at least be likened to a respectable Chablis. The virtues of this air are not confined to its bracing effects; it has also a direct action on the landscape. The clarity of the atmosphere and the frequent wide expanses of luminous sky give a depth and distance to a country view which are not often to be found in other lands; it takes a middle course, as it were, between the softness of English and the hard brilliance of Spanish outlines. This translucent quality has influenced the work of French artists to a marked degree; it is notice-able in their painting at all periods, but at none so clearly as with the Impressionist school of the nineteenth century. There is a particular radiance in its landscapes which could have been captured nowhere except in France, and is outstanding in the work of such artists as Monet, Boudin, Sisley, and Pissarro; but perhaps with none of this school is it so acutely felt as in the pictures of the young Englishman who spent the greater part of his short painting life in France at the beginning of the nineteenth century : Richard Parkes Bonington.

The climate of a country directly affects the characteristics of the inhabitants. The French are hard-working and clear-thinking; the bracing air makes them strong and energetic, and stimulates them mentally to a highly developed standard of common sense. This excellent quality is, indeed, sometimes carried to extreme lengths, and, except amongst those with Celtic blood, one often misses in this highly sane outlook the imagination and feeling for romanticism which is to be found amongst the inhabitants of cloudy countries.

These, of course, are obviously generalisations, since in a land so large as France there are many sorts of climate, landscape, and inhabitants: indeed there is no country in Europe which covers such wide extremes. We in England are under the happy impression that our countryside has many aspects, and it is with astonished disappointment that we discover that these differences are lost on foreign visitors. They may visit the Lake District and Salisbury Plain, the Weald of Kent and the Yorkshire moors, but to them all seems cast in the same mould, all is typically English. We are presumably in the position of a shepherd with his flock; to us each sheep has its outstanding characteristics, to the stranger all appear as alike as peas.

In France, however, the most unobservant traveller cannot fail to notice the striking differences in landscape. The horrid plains of the North and the sunny olive-groves of the South have as little in common as the vine-clad country in the West and the Alpine scenery of Savoy in the East. It is not surprising, with this wide choice of landscape and climate at their door, that the French prefer to stay at home rather than to travel in foreign countries, since not only have they some of the loveliest scenery in Europe, but they can also boast the finest range of architecture outside Italy. They have, indeed, been treated so lavishly by fortune that they show a tendency to be spoiled thereby, particularly in regard to their understanding of foreign nations. This is roughly paralleled by the effect the almost worldwide use of English has on an Englishman's command of foreign languages: it causes an atrophy of certain faculties which would be better exercised.

If the French outlook towards foreign countries seems sometimes open to criticism, there can never be anything but praise for the manner in which the domestic life of the nation is organised. By comparison, the methods of the Anglo-Saxon races are little short of barbarous. Life in France is conceived on logical lines: a Frenchman, for instance, can eat, drink, or buy tobacco when, where, and how he pleases. There are no bewildering restrictions such as those in

England, which force the modest drinker either to waste his last glass of wine or fling it down his throat in unseemly haste. A proper consideration is given to the art of eating and drinking. Irrespective of class, the midday meal is recognised as the most important function in the day, one which should be carried through with proper dignity and leisure. Where in England the lunch interval for the working or professional classes is seldom prolonged beyond one hour, in France the hours from midday until two o'clock are wherever possible devoted scrupulously to the serious business of eating. To the traveller, this excellent custom is sometimes rather irritating. If he has perhaps no more than a few hours to spend in a town, it is particularly thwarting to find that churches, museums, and many shops are shut like traps on the stroke of twelve; the time available for sightseeing may thus be practically extinguished. He will be well advised, however, to follow the habits of the country and, forgetting art and architecture, partake of an enormous meal instead.

The French are an essentially temperate people, but nevertheless they would never consider eating a meal without the accompaniment of wine; no child is too young, no dotard too old to drink a glass of wine with his food. To a new-comer to the country, café life, which is such a feature of French towns, might suggest a certain alcoholic abandon; nothing, however, could be further from the truth. A whole family, in the highest of spirits, may occupy a table for the whole of a Sunday afternoon on nothing stronger, or more remunerative to the proprietor, than a few glasses of coffee. This economical expenditure must prove a serious drawback to café owners. When one observes the crowded cafés of Paris or other large towns one is apt to think at first what a richly rewarded profession this must be; on reflection, however, one wonders how they succeed in obtaining any return at all.

Fortunately, the cares of café proprietors are not one's business, and, beyond proving a better client than one's neighbour, one can forget them in the extraordinary charm and interest of spending a little time in one of the more popular of these resorts. They are usually placed in the most animated centre of the town, so that all the life there may be, whether the throngs of Paris or marketing peasants up from the country, pass before one in an animated parade. Such an arrangement in England would probably cause acute embarrassment, and self-conscious pedestrians would make long detours to avoid running the gauntlet of hundreds of critical eyes. The French have no such weakness, and appreciate their part in the play; whether with the players or with the audience, they respond quite naturally to the best of their abilities. They are fortunate in having little of the inferiority

4 Village Café

5 The Ice-Cream Stall

6   On the Way to Market

7   A National Sport : Bicycle-racing

8　Cattle Fair

9　A National Pastime : Bowls

10 Restocking the Café

11 The Apéritif

complex which plays such havoc with Anglo-Saxon self-esteem, and this is particularly noticeable in the women. An English girl unblessed by nature almost immediately abandons the struggle to present a personable appearance, and is satisfied to be looked on as a "good sort." Frenchwomen, however, hold the opposite point of view: the less the endowment the greater the effort; and such a gift have they for presenting themselves in the best light that the ugly will often eclipse the pretty and well-formed. The fault probably lies with the Englishman (or at best it is a vicious circle in which the blame can be equally divided between the sexes), since he fails to supply the essential encouragement of personal interest which the Frenchman lavishes so spontaneously on the women of his country.

Indeed, the contrast between the two nations applies to both sexes, and the Frenchman is continually amazed not only by the Englishman's apparent aloofness towards his womenkind, particularly in public, but also by his love of segregation amongst his fellow-men. Clubs, in the English sense of the word, are practically unknown in France, and the dignified rows of these institutions which line St. James's Street and Pall Mall, together with their complacent occupants, cause far more astonishment to the average Frenchman than would the most abandoned scene in a *boîte* in Montmartre (if, indeed, it could ever take place) to the most respectable member of a London club.

The presence of a woman at a Frenchman's table is perhaps equally essential as that of a glass of wine, and a "stag" party, either in public or private, is regarded by him as a most boring and unnecessary function. This attitude is, of course, the result of a very different education from the Englishman's; the French, being immune from the monastic atmosphere of the English public school and university, learn to appreciate ladies at a much earlier age. When in England the Frenchman is staggered by the docility of women in leaving the table before the men at the end of dinner, and, in company with the nationals of other Latin countries, he considers the custom of the men lingering round the port and brandy both barbaric and a waste of time.

The gaiety of the cafés of Paris and the big industrial towns might lead the visitor to expect a similar state of affairs in the provinces, with small-town cafés a clatter of animated citizens up to eleven o'clock or midnight. Except in the South, however, there is little abandon of this sort, and, although the cafés may still be open, they are usually absolutely deserted at an hour far earlier than the closing-time of an English pub. The same may be said of the streets, which by ten o'clock are practically empty.

There is another feature of French life which is worth mentioning:

the excellence of the beds. One may travel all over the country, staying in large hotels and small, and it will be an exceptional misfortune to pass a single night in an uncomfortable bed; while the hygiene with which the careful housewife festoons the balconies of her house with bedclothes, so that they may be exposed to sunshine and air, is wholly admirable. In the kitchen and in the bedroom, indeed, the *mère de famille* is paramount, and with full and capable control of these two essential departments she needs no vote to rule the country.

The average Frenchman of the middle and lower classes neither has nor apparently needs many amusements to break the monotony of family life, and any desire for distraction is adequately gratified by the simple pastime of bowls. It is a game which is played to a considerable degree in the North, but in the Midi, that indefinite area covering roughly the southern quarter of France, it seems to fill every vacant minute. The method of play has only a rough resemblance to the English game, while the site of play has seldom any resemblance whatever. Just as no spare time appears too short to practise a throw, so no place is too restricted, no surface too uneven, no spot too inconvenient to carry on the game. If there is no dusty verge available, then the highroad itself will serve, and players must scatter left and right to let a car pass through. These delays and hazards probably add interest to the game, and they certainly create a considerable diversion in a motor drive on a summer evening.

Bowls undoubtedly takes first place as the national recreation, but the sport, if such it can be called, which perhaps excites the greatest interest throughout the country, an interest paralleled by those of football and cricket in England, is bicycle-racing. Some of these races are merely local, but there are more important international contests in which the course entails a circuit of the whole country; thus the inhabitants of remote districts have all the excitement of, for example, a visit to Epsom Downs without even moving from their doors.

The participants are national heroes to an even greater degree than their footballing and cricketing counterparts in England, and are received with the wildest enthusiasm in the course of their rides. The excitement in a small village through which a race is to pass is intense, and streets and windows are crowded for long before the competitors are due to arrive. At last they come, in groups of three or four strung out over a long distance, thin men with tense, strained faces and enormous, muscular legs pedalling for dear life; if the weather is wet they are so covered with mud that the large numerals tied to their backs become invisible, and the heroes pass unrecognised. Their laurels are certainly dearly won.

Another sport which lies close to the heart of the majority of Frenchmen is fishing. It is a pastime which is no doubt encouraged by wives, since it provides both an innocuous recreation and also the possibility of a free addition to the dinner-table. On rocks by the seashore, on piers and jetties, on the banks of rivers and by lakesides, wherever, in fact, there is water, there also will be found a number of engrossed fishermen. But whether fishing in salt water or in fresh, the sportsmen appear to be seldom rewarded, and one fears that French waters are now as sparsely stocked with fish as the greater part of the countryside is with game.

Bowls, bicycling and fishing, then, are three of the principal recreations, but there is an enthusiasm, falling almost into the category of a pastime, which transcends all of these: a passionate interest in the formalities of death. A man may be abused or neglected in life, but he may be sure of an infinite popularity in death, an encouraging thought which must have brought comfort to many obscure and unsuccessful individuals. Where *pompes funèbres* are concerned the usual thrift is forgotten, and no expense will be spared to give the departed a farewell enhanced by all the sable trappings of waving plumes and long-tailed horses.

The funeral is conducted with great ceremony, but the most interesting formality comes as the coffin leaves the church at the end of the service. The hearse takes up a position about fifty yards from the church door; the mourners then file out and form two lines, men to the right, women to the left, while lastly come the members of the family, the faces of the women concealed under veils of flowing black, who take their places in two groups near the coffin. An orator then steps forward and delivers a spirited eulogy on the merits of the departed, while the family mourners, overcome by the moving words, dab their eyes with handkerchiefs held in black-gloved hands. The corpse, beneath his mound of wreaths, might well be wondering why this appreciation of his outstanding qualities had been so carefully concealed during life!

The speech having reached its graceful climax, the mourners shake hands with the family, and the hearse leaves for the cemetery at a cheerful trot.

But expense does not end with the funeral; the grave has still to be surmounted by a suitable monument. Pride of family and probably affection for the departed demand that it shall rival, if it cannot outshine, its neighbours in the churchyard. In large cemeteries, such as that of Père La Chaise in Paris, competition is carried to remarkable lengths, and the steep slopes of the Father's former garden, overlooking Paris, bristle with large stone monuments, mostly designed in a very startling taste. Much the same state of affairs is found in country graveyards, which are often made unnecessarily hideous by the size and bombast of the memorial crosses and by the unfortunately popular wreaths of purple metal or bead flowers.

The interior of the church itself on a Sunday morning may somewhat surprise the average English visitor, whether or not he shares the religious views of the majority of the French people. On entering, he will be rather shocked at being expected to pay for one of the wood-and-wicker *prie-Dieu*, which are usually piled in a corner and guarded by a bent but active old woman in weeds, who will demand twenty-five centimes before handing over one of these remarkably uncomfortable contraptions either for the sitting or kneeling position. The visitor, however, should be careful not to give her a franc with a generous wave of the hand, since, although it will be hastily accepted, she will despise the donor for this profligate exhibition of wealth. Having secured his *prie-Dieu*, the Englishman will feel inclined to pick it up and put it discreetly by some pillar in the back of the church. This action would again earn the scorn of the onlooker, since, in place of thus effacing himself, he should drag the *prie-Dieu* with the maximum of noise across the stone floor, and place it with determination as near the altar as he can.

The attitude of the congregation, and indeed of the clergy as well, may also surprise the visitor during the service. Although the latter will be conducted with reverence, the diversity in general appearance of the canons in the choir, despite the similarity of clerical costume, and their obvious reluctance or inability to form an orderly procession, when the occasion demands, are striking evidence of the strong individuality of the French. This criticism, however, does not apply to the verger, delightfully called the "Suisse"; he is, indeed, a dignified and magnificent figure, dressed in a purple mantle and a black velvet hat of Napoleonic design. The great stick he carries, ornamented with a massive silver boss, is the symbol of his office and clear evidence of his ability to keep order in the congregation.

Perhaps the worshippers present an even more striking example than the clergy of the admirable quality of individualism. The Englishman's eagerness to conform in public is unknown in France; while in a church of any denomination in England the spectacle of one member of the congregation standing when the others are on their knees, would cause a general feeling of discomfort, a similar action in France would pass entirely unnoticed. Thus even in their devotions the French give yet another proof of their love of liberty and innate common sense

12 A Cemetery

13 Sunday Morning

The vagaries of French taste come as a perpetual surprise to visitors from other countries. During the eighteenth century the standard of achievement in almost every branch of art reached a perfection which was unequalled anywhere else in Europe. In the following century, however, when universal decay set in, France rushed with truly Latin impetuosity helter-skelter down the scale until, at about the time of the fall of the Second Empire, she found herself in an outstanding position at the opposite extreme. These strictures, of course, can only be said to apply to popular art, but it is this unfortunately which leaves its concrete manifestations in every town as witnesses to contemporary taste. For the intelligentsia there was an unbroken succession of splendid painters, while in literature the famous figures probably equalled in talent and certainly exceeded in number the giants of the previous century. Nor must we forget the magnificent culmination to the art of the century provided by the School of the Impressionists, which emerged, unique and triumphant, above the surrounding horrors of the age.

The depth, however, to which taste had sunk is, perhaps, best exemplified in the monuments and statues with which squares and public gardens were, and still are, freely decorated. The first thought aroused by these objects is the extraordinary good fortune of the sculptors in finding a market for their formidable marbles; the second that their good fortune hardly compensates for the pain caused to the public, which cannot avoid seeing their works. Probably the worst monuments are those raised to the memory of Gambetta, of which there is an example in almost every town. A comprehensive volume of reproductions of these might provide a useful warning of what to avoid when erecting a memorial to a public figure.

The French have a custom, which we do not share, of renaming their streets after anyone they particularly wish to compliment. It is a favour usually reserved for the dead, but occasionally this rule is relaxed, as in the case of Mr. Chamberlain, when it is wished to give immediate effect to great public enthusiasm. By means of this custom it may not be extravagant to assess the relative popularity of modern historical figures; the more frequent the recurrence of a name, the greater the esteem. For first place there is no competition, one name stands isolated far before all others: Gambetta. But the next half-dozen places are less easy to fill correctly, and the following are only tentatively suggested: Thiers, Foch, Jean Jaurés, Victor Hugo, President Wilson, Carnot. The President has the distinction of being the only foreigner to reach these heights, while his French colleague at the Versailles Conference, Monsieur Clemenceau, would come much

2

14 (*opposite*)
The Weekly Wash

further down the list. One fears that the English member of the peace-making triumvirate has, owing to longevity, lost all chance of being commemorated by even so much as a *cul-de-sac*.

There is so much that is beautiful to be found in France that it is difficult to know whether the towns or the countryside deserve greater praise: the one varies as much as the other. The cool grey cities of the North are as unlike the white-painted, tree-shaded towns of the South as are the landscapes in which each are set. To travellers from northern countries, the southern towns have a special charm; while such places as Beauvais or Caen have distinct affinities with York or Salisbury, the towns of the Midi provide the stimulus of something entirely divorced from life in the North. Everyone must feel the excitement of these sunbaked cities, in which narrow streets, often so blocked by the great trunks of century-old plane-trees that two cars can barely pass, open into shaded squares, with splashing fountains and many cafés in which the tables are set under striped awnings or beneath canopies of pleached trees. The inhabitants have a natural gift for adding to the picturesqueness of the scene; the open-air markets, for example, turn the streets or squares in which they are held into a blaze of colour. Fruit and vegetables are piled high in shining heaps, and barrows are laden with every sort of flower, from the wild to the exotic; even the carcasses of pigs are sometimes given a wreath of flowers to clothe their pink nakedness. With all this beauty goes a babel of bargaining and backchat which is stupefying to those who are not inured to it, and it may be something of a relief to pass out of the town again into the quiet of the countryside.

The French are not particularly sensitive to noise; indeed, on the whole, they would seem to prefer it to quiet, since to them it has a certain stimulating quality. A restaurant, for example, cannot be full enough or hot enough to please its patrons, since noise and heat typify success; the same, up to a point, may be said of towns in the extreme South, where there is only the shortest pause during the night in the normal sounds of the streets. Marseilles, with its trams scream-ing up and down the Cannebière for twenty hours a day, easily wins the prize for the noisiest town in the country, and perhaps in the world, but there is a considerable number of rivals for the position of runner-up. The noise of the streets, however, is the only serious drawback to the larger cities; apart from this, almost every one of them, whether it is predominantly an artistic or an industrial centre, is exceedingly pleasant and profitable to stay in, while many which are renowned only for their commercial products contain buildings or museums which are richly rewarding to inspect.

15   "Route Nationale"

16   Sculpture : Eighteenth-century, at Nîmes

17   Sculpture : Nineteenth-century, at Amiens (in honour of Jules Verne)

18   The Corn Harvest in Normandy

19   Haystacks in the Dauphiné

20   Fishermen, St. Tropez

21   On the Quays, Marseilles

The beauties of the countryside spring so clearly to the eye that they require no praise to make them widely appreciated. Even the hardened town-lover is almost bound to find something in the rich diversity of landscape to please him, whether it is the mountainous scenery of the French Alps or the wooded valleys of the great rivers which flow through the northern half of the country, the intimate beauty of the Dordogne or perhaps the olive- and pine-clad hills of Provence, where blue sky and sea, red earth and green or silvery trees form so lovely a union. Almost every traveller will discover some district which especially appeals to him, some favourite and perhaps little-known part of the countryside to which he will always wish to return.

It is fortunate that the least attractive parts of the country are in the North, so that the tourist, landing at a Channel port, can cross the wide dull plains while the scenery is still new to him, and while the long, tree-lined roads stretching away over an agricultural landscape, which is so surprisingly large in scale, have still the interest of novelty. But even the unromantic districts have a certain charm, which springs probably from a feeling of essential genuineness. In the Home Counties of England, by contrast, the landscape is apt to wear a spurious air, as if it were only being kept alive by artificial means. The heathery commons are crossed by asphalt paths, the bosky woods are sprinkled with neo-Tudor cottages: at first glance it is country; at the second it is, alas, only suburbia.

The French are fortunate to be spared these troubles of over-population; there are, indeed, many hundreds of square miles where there is barely sufficient peasantry adequately to till the soil. It is an economic misfortune which often has the minor compensating advantage of giving the landscape its grand, desolate look of open fields extending to a distant horizon unbroken by any sign of habitation or human life. From this frequent aspect of desertion it might be expected that farming would be neglected, but this, on the whole, is not the case. Although the density of population is low, the standard of industry is remarkably high; and all the national thrift is exercised in utilising every square yard of soil to the full. This is not surprising in the noted agricultural districts, but it becomes very impressive in the many rocky regions where the difficulties of cultivation would seem to outweigh the possibility of any return. On the stony slopes of Provence, for example, or still more in the sterile valleys of the Alps, where every pocket of earth, however small, is put to some use, it must entail the most strenuous labour to produce even a modest profit.

Tradition is strong with the French peasant, and he clings tenaciously to his antiquated principles in preference to the labour-saving methods of modern science. In some directions there has been no change for centuries. One of the most familiar sights as one passes through the country, for example, is a peasant woman keeping a long vigil over a single cow while it munches the communal grass bordering the sides of the road. Fodder is expensive, but time is extremely cheap. It is this unhurried feeling which pervades the pastoral lands and gives an ageless, immutable character to those who spend their lives in the cultivation of the soil.

The art of forestry is particularly well understood in France. Whether the trees are grown purely for timber, as in the great forests south of the Seine and in the neighbourhood of the town of Vierzon, or for beauty along roads or in town squares, they are as carefully tended as if they were ornaments to a private park. The French have an innate gift for picturesque planting, inherited, perhaps, from the great garden-makers of the early eighteenth century, who with their quincunxes and groves created scenes of beauty which have never been surpassed. Almost all the main roads are planted with avenues of trees—elm, acacia, chestnut, and lime alternating with the more usual plane. The latter is the loveliest and, at the same time, the most practical; the pale, smooth trunks gracefully frame, without obscuring, the passing scenery, while the thick viridian foliage shades the road from the hot summer sunshine. In Normandy and in some parts of Burgundy fruit-trees take the place of forest trees and give colour and beauty, if little shade, to the highway. Tracts of country which are either too wet or too dry for cultivation, but have some depth of soil, are also given up to the growing of timber. Marshy water-meadows by streams and rivers are planted with groves of poplars or willows, while arid districts such as the sandy wastes south of Bordeaux and the rocky hills along the Mediterranean coast support vast forests of pine-trees. In the art of arboriculture England has much to learn from France.

For those who prefer a discreet mixture of architecture with landscape, there are the innumerable châteaux which can be visited by the public; in addition to the famous buildings on the Loire, the majority of which are now museums rather than inhabited houses, there is a large quantity of country houses of great architectural merit which are well worth seeing. Indeed, to many a tour of the lesser-known châteaux will be just as interesting as a tour of the cathedrals, and in addition the natural curiosity as to how other nations live will be at least partially assuaged by seeing the interiors of their houses.

In England the country house is one of our most successful products, but the French are no more than a short way behind us, although the quantity in proportion to the size of the country is much smaller. The surroundings of the houses, the gardens and parks, reach a far higher standard in England, but in the architecture and the contents there is little to choose. The English are on the whole more wealthy, and their houses are consequently better maintained, but perhaps we can hardly claim great credit for this. The French have an advantage in the quantity of running water which is so often available for the making of formal gardens in the manner of Le Nôtre, or, as was often done long after all need for defence was past, for feeding a wide moat round the house. Those moats are sometimes so beautifully contrived that the house has the appearance of a majestic ship floating on the waters of a formal lake. It is an effect that is only rarely emulated in England.

The interiors of many châteaux are extraordinarily rich and beautiful, and those who may not care for French furniture when exported from its country can hardly fail to appreciate its high quality when seen in a proper setting of panelled or tapestried rooms. The arrangement of the furniture is usually very different from that to be found in a parallel house in England. There are invariably a great quantity of upright chairs, suggesting large animated parties, but furniture designed for repose is never seen. Often the chairs are set round a vast circular table covered with a heavy fringed cloth which is placed in the middle of the room, considerably to the detriment of its appearance, and round which a large circle of guests can be conveniently disposed. Indeed, in the majority of châteaux the rooms conform in their arrangement to a mid-nineteenth-century convention which has been little altered during the passing years.

The long coastline of France supplies as large a variety of scenery as is to be found inland. There are the white cliffs of the Channel coast which merge into the harsh black rocks of northern Brittany; the southern side of the peninsula facing the Bay of Biscay strikes a more gentle note, with long expanses of sand broken by the bays and indentations of the low shore. The many miles of coast extending from the mouth of the Loire to the Spanish frontier are not particularly attractive and are rarely punctuated by seaside resorts, Royan, Arcachon, and Biarritz being the only pleasure towns of any size. It is, however, to the Mediterranean coast that the sun-lover turns, where, for all its popularity, there are still many deserted beaches on which pinewoods grow close to the water's edge and rocky points protect the bather from the mistral wind. For the gregarious there are the crowded bathing-resorts east of Cannes, where during a successful season the rocks and sand are so thickly covered with a cosmopolitan collection of baked bodies that it may be difficult to find a space to sit; while for those who prefer a typically French atmosphere there are the many little ports and fishing villages between Marseilles and Toulon, where worthy bourgeois families pass their summer holidays, moving with little change of costume from their parlour in some provincial town to the burning sands of the beach.

Whatever form a holiday in France may take, whether it is based on a tour through the countryside, an urban round of cathedrals and picture-galleries, or a bathing orgy in the sunshine, the traveller will certainly return invigorated and stimulated both in mind and body; a little increase in girth will possibly be compensated by a parallel expansion in the mental outlook and, perhaps, by a wider understanding of the French point of view. It is the object of this book to encourage the traveller from other countries to explore the beauties of France, and to fill in for himself the details of a picture which is here only lightly indicated.

22 Summer at Antibes : Eden Rock

23   Apple-blossom in Normandy

CHAPTER II

NORMANDY AND THE BRETON PENINSULA

THE three provinces of Normandy, Brittany, and Maine form together a fairly compact group. The long coastline to the Channel stretches from Tréport, a short way beyond Dieppe, in the north to the western point of Brittany, which projects far out into the Atlantic, while the remaining boundaries follow a nearly constant arc along the southern coast of Brittany to a position just south of the mouth of the Loire, and so inland in a wide sweep northward between Paris and the coast.

Although so closely united geographically, Normandy and Brittany differ greatly in character. The former is a rich pastoral country with all the appearance, perhaps fallacious, of agricultural prosperity, emphasised by plump cattle and plump peasants, while the rugged, windswept landscape of Brittany suggests poverty and the hard struggle which, at least in the north, the inhabitants have in order to wring a precarious livelihood from an ungenerous soil.

These two provinces have for decades exerted a strong attraction on the less adventurous British tourist, and it is an attraction which is readily understandable, since for the seeker after a pretty countryside, which is in general the English taste, there is none to be found in a foreign land more accessible than Normandy and Brittany. In addition, the historical connection of Normandy with England is a further inducement for a visit, while the very name of Brittany inspires a certain confidence in the inexperienced traveller.

In any case, the English are fortunate to have this country so easily within reach, since Normandy contains not only lovely country but also several extremely interesting towns, and Brittany has at least a romantic coastline and a rugged beauty of landscape which will appeal to all admirers of Cornwall or Scotland. The small province of Maine, though less spectacular than its two neighbours, has a fine capital in Le Mans and a gentle countryside which is essentially French in character.

As a general rule, a race of people takes its name from the country which it inhabits, but in Normandy the usual process was reversed and the province was called after the Northmen, or Normans, who descended upon it from Scandinavia during the ninth century. This wild and energetic race created such havoc in the country bordering the Seine that the French found it prudent to adopt a policy of appeasement, and in 911, by the Treaty of St. Clair-sur-Epte, King Charles the Simple handed over to Rollo, chief of the Normans, an area corresponding roughly to the province of Normandy. The line of robust dukes founded by Rollo prospered during the following century and added considerably to their territorial importance. Duke Robert, known as the Magnificent, or, less flatteringly, the Devil (1027–1035), died on a pilgrimage to Jerusalem, leaving as heir his illegitimate son William, who was destined to play such an important part in English history.

Normandy is now subdivided into five departments, the most northerly of which, Seine-Inférieure, is bounded on the north by the little river Bresle, while on the south it is almost detached from the remainder of the province by the river Seine, which zigzags wildly towards the sea at Le Havre. The landscape of the department has nothing in common with that of the southern parts of Normandy, and is more closely allied to the plains of Picardy, but in a more softened form. It is a country of low uplands and vast, unhedged, arable fields, varied here and there by great stretches of beechwoods which form a beautiful and welcome break in the undulating countryside. The first impression is one of space, and this is particularly noticeable to anyone coming fresh from the little fields and high hedges of England.

Towards the northern extremity of the smooth coastline of low white cliffs lies Dieppe, a curious town of dual personality. Along the wide sea-front rise the casino and the big hotels which were built when the town achieved a sudden wave of fashionable popularity towards the end of the last century, while behind this elegant barricade lie the narrow streets and attractive houses and churches of the old town, grouping at one end of the harbour. The season at Dieppe is gay but rather short, and for the greater part of the year the inhabitants retire to the sheltered intimacy of the old town, and abandon the long line of shuttered windows on the sea-front to complete desolation.

At its southern extremity the front is closed by a great barrier of cliff, on the point of which stands a castle, a picturesque group of towers dating from the fifteenth century; it replaces a twelfth-century castle which is said to have been built by Henry II of England. The early history of the town consists principally of disasters: frequent sieges, a seventeenth-century plague in which many thousands died, an attack in 1694 by the Anglo-Dutch fleet from which it took many years to recover, and so forth. It must therefore have been with almost incredulous delight that this unlucky town found itself at the restoration of the Bourbons becoming a fashionable and prosperous resort owing to the patronage of the Duchesse de Berry, who suddenly discovered the merits of sea-bathing. It was soon after given increased royal *cachet* by the presence of Louis-Philippe and his queen a few miles away at the Château d'Eu, the fascinating but hideous interior of which remains materially unaltered since the days when Queen Victoria was entertained there. This château gives perhaps a more accurate impression of the life of the Orléans monarch than any other building in France.

The other large port on the coast of this maritime department is Le Havre, which lies on the point of land where the wide mouth of the Seine opens to the sea. It is a larger town than Dieppe and is planned on a more spacious scale, with big squares and boulevards which group agreeably around the inner basins of the docks. Architecturally there is little of importance with the exception of the curious church of Notre Dame near the quays at the southern point of the town; it was built between the years 1574 and 1638, and varies in style from bad gothic to robust Renaissance, the shell belonging to the former but the doorways and other decorative detail to the latter.

As the Seine nears the sea the banks open out, so that for the last part of its course the estuary reaches a width of six or seven miles. Along the northern bank stretch flat fields, half meadow, half marsh, which merge into a long chain of limestone cliffs running parallel to the river. On these cliffs are little villages, clinging like barnacles to the rocks, in which caves are often used as habitations. Some of the villages are more considerable; Tancarville, for example, contains a fine mediæval and eighteenth-century castle, from the terrace of which there is a magnificent view across the river to the low hills of the department of Eure. A few miles further up the river, in the little village of Vieux-Port, is a twelfth-century chapel dedicated to St. Thomas à Beckett. The two banks of the Seine are connected by a number of ferries which vary considerably in size and apparent security, but there is no bridge below Rouen, which is nearly sixty miles from Le Havre.

On the rising country to the north of the river lie a number of towns of some size: Harfleur, Bolbec, Yvetot, Caudebec, all with gothic churches and streets of agreeable stuccoed houses, but little else of particular interest, except perhaps Harfleur, which boasts a monument to Jehan de Grouchy, who drove the English out of the town in 1435. Towards Rouen the country becomes more picturesque, with steep slopes covered with deciduous trees, but it is a populous district much marred by buildings, since modern French cottages can rival anything in England for hideousness. Through this landscape of trees and houses

one descends to Rouen, which lies on a wide bend of the river surrounded by considerable chalk hills.

The commercial suburbs of the town are enormous, extending far on
both sides of the river, but the old town forms a compact area on the
northern bank.   In spite of the crowded animation of the streets and
the great activity of the quays, Rouen bears a somewhat melancholy
air, as if the spirit of the martyred Joan of Arc were still brooding over
the town.   The streets are rather narrow and are bordered by tall
houses which restrict the sunlight; the stonework of the cathedral,
the Hôtel de Ville, and other public buildings has a dark and gloomy
surface; it very often rains.   But as one paddles about the wet streets
one may see from beneath one's umbrella a considerable number of
buildings of architectural interest.   There is the cathedral, which is
described in another chapter, and the Palais de Justice, a splendid
gothic building dating from the beginning of the sixteenth century,
but much marred by forbidding nineteenth-century additions; there
is also an extensive and rather interesting picture-gallery.   But
perhaps the most pleasing buildings are the old houses dating from the
fifteenth and sixteenth centuries which are to be seen in many parts of
the town.   Some are built in stone, but the more attractive are the
timbered houses with projecting gables and a riot of carving.   One of
the latter has been turned into a restaurant, so that the tourist can conveniently observe the well-restored interior as he consumes an
excellent meal.

East of Rouen, on the boundary of Normandy and the Île-de-France,
is the agreeable little town of Gisors, the castle of which was partly
built by Henry I and Henry II of England; it is now a vast and impressive
ruin.   A high and well-preserved curtain-wall, which breaks at regular
intervals into towers, encloses an area of several acres in the centre of
which rises a steep mound on which stands the octagonal keep surrounded by a protective circle of bastions and towers.   The ruins now
form a public garden of which any town might well be proud.   The
other building of interest in Gisors is the cathedral, which is an astonishing medley of styles from Romanesque to Renaissance.   The
incompleted south-west tower is the most interesting part, and is an
unusually beautiful and delicate example of the transition from gothic
to the classical style; in the interior there is a fascinating spiral staircase
dating from the same period.

From Gisors the river Epte, which forms the boundary of the department of Eure, flows southward into the wooded valley of the Seine.
Beyond, between Evreux and Louviers, with its amusing church
in *flamboyant* fifteenth-century gothic, stretches an area of thickly

24   Rouen from the Cathedral, looking to the Church of St. Ouen

25   Caen from the Cathedral

26 An Old Street in Rouen

27 The Way to
the Cathedral,
Lisieux

wooded country through which runs the river Eure.   The Forest of
Bord lies between these two towns, while further west extend mile
upon mile of well-ordered beechwoods.   Long rides, cut through
the woods, radiate from circular open spaces; thus the eye is
carried in every direction down interminable avenues into the heart of
the forest.   Beechwoods have the merit of looking lovely at all times
of the year; they are as beautiful in the pale green of spring as they are
in the russet of autumn, but perhaps they are at their best in the delicate
silver and brown of winter.

As one passes from the department of Eure into Calvados the
country takes on the aspect which is particularly associated with
Normandy.   The small broken hills are divided by high hedges into
patches of bright green meadow; all about these meadows are planted
apple-trees, beneath which graze well-fed black-and-white cattle and
flocks of sheep.   Here, without doubt, the season to see the country is
spring, when the apple-trees are in blossom and the otherwise unspec-
tacular countryside breaks out into an almost musical-comedy pretti-
ness.   In its more sober moments the country is curiously like
England, with its small-scale undulations and high thorn hedges along
the roads—so like, indeed, that the architecture of the farms and
cottages comes as a considerable shock.   At its best, the Normandy
style of timbered building has some affinity with English Tudor,
although the practice of painting the timbers a dark red-brown is
particularly unfortunate; but at its worst the Third Republic replicas
are even more hideous than their by-pass counterparts in this country.

Apple-trees and cows indicate accurately the two principal products
of the district: cider, with its derivative in liqueur form, Calvados,
and cheese.   The former is the drink of the country, and in this area
takes the place for the poorer classes of wine; there is also a considerable consumption of the very excellent Calvados.   Cheese is in a
rather different class, since it is made all over France; indeed, it is
computed that no fewer than five hundred varieties are produced in
different parts of the country.   But Normandy is the principal lactic
country, and can boast the most famous of all cheeses, the Camembert.
It was first made in a little village of that name four miles from Vimout-
iers by Marie Harel in 1761, whose memory is now perpetuated by a
monument in the main square, erected in 1929.   While Madame
Harel was inventing her cheese at Camembert, a woman who was to
have fame of a very different order was born a few miles away at Les
Champeaux: Charlotte Corday.

In the undistinguished little town of Pont l'Evêque, between
Honfleur and Lisieux, is made another renowned cheese, and nearby at

Livarot an excellent but lesser known variety.   Also, the majority of
the fresh cream cheeses are made in this district, such as Petit Suisse,
Neufchâtel, Bonde, Gournay, and many others.

The department of Calvados also contains a group of interesting and
historical towns: Lisieux, Caen, Bayeux, and Falaise, the latter three of
which are closely connected with the history of the Norman Kings of
England.   Until the last years of the nineteenth century Lisieux was
a quiet market-town with a fine gothic cathedral, a particularly handsome bishop's palace, and a large number of picturesque timbered
houses.   The latter are as fine as any in France, and some of the streets,
such as the narrow rue aux Fèvres, in which the projecting gables
almost meet across the street, remain materially unaltered since the
sixteenth century.   The death, however, in 1897 of Sister Theresa, a
young Carmelite nun, was destined to alter the whole aspect of the
town.   It was soon reported that miraculous cures had been effected on
those who had prayed on the nun's grave in the cemetery, and as the
fame increased more and more pilgrims came to Lisieux.   In 1923
Theresa was canonised, and her remains were removed from the
obscure grave in the cemetery and brought for burial to the Carmelite
convent.   On a steep slope on the south side of the town a vast
basilica, designed in the French casino style, is now nearing completion,
while the roads up to it are lined with the endless little shops which
inevitably arise near any place of pilgrimage.   Religious emblems and
Calvados are, indeed, the two main products of the town, and almost
every shop is devoted to the sale of one or the other, while many
prudently combine the two.   The bountiful St. Theresa has brought
great prosperity to her home town.

West of Lisieux lies Caen, which William the Conqueror made his
principal place of residence and which owes to him three of its main
buildings: the castle, now a ruin, the Abbaye-aux-Hommes, and the
Abbaye-aux-Dames.   The two latter stand as twin sentinels on either
side of the town.   They were built at the instigation of Pope Leo IX,
who declined to recognise the marriage of William to Matilda, daughter
of Baldwin, Count of Flanders, unless they each built an abbey.   In the
Abbaye-aux-Dames both were buried, but the tomb of the Conqueror
was destroyed at the Revolution, and all trace of his remains has disappeared.   The coffin of Matilda, however, was concealed in the
garden of the adjoining convent and was later returned to the church,
where it now reposes in the choir under a monument dating from 1813.

In the neighbouring town of Bayeux is kept the famous tapestry which
is associated with the name of Matilda, and which was given by her to
her brother-in-law, who was bishop of that see.   This needlework

picture is not tapestry in the usually accepted term, but is formed by sewing coloured cloth on to a white linen background. There are fifty-eight animated scenes, taking the story from the moment when Edward the Confessor decided to bequeath the crown of England to the Duke of Normandy until the victory of William at Hastings. The figures are depicted in the liveliest hues with little attempt at realism, the horses, for example, being as often purple or green as any of the more usually accepted colours. The magnificent cathedral, partly Romanesque, partly gothic, the old stone houses and steep cobbled streets make Bayeux an extremely picturesque town.

The birthplace of the Conqueror, or the Bastard, as he was called during his early years, was the castle at Falaise which lies on the hills near the southern border of Calvados. Only the keep and the Talbot Tower now rise from amongst the ruined walls and defences on the summit of a steep hill above the town. In a small windowless cell hollowed out of the walls of the former, which are five yards thick, William was born in 1027 to Arlette, the daughter of a tanner. Looking down from the walls one can see far below at the foot of the hill the sheds and yards of a small tannery which is still working in the same place as when Arlette mounted the hill to take her somewhat equivocal place in the pedigree of the English kings.

It is perhaps interesting to note that to the French William is known as the Conqueror not for his exploits in England but rather for his prowess on the death of his father in securing Normandy, to which, as a bastard, he had only a doubtful claim.

As Calvados gives way to the large province of Orne, the landscape assumes a less typically Normandy aspect; the scale increases, and long, gently undulating hills, on which the pasture is broken by hedges but few trees, alternate with large areas of forest country. Although rather poor in scenery, the department is rich in domestic architecture and contains a dozen or more châteaux of unusual merit. There is Carrouges, for example, between Alençon and Argenton, with its beautiful sixteenth-century gatehouse and walls of rose-red brick which rise from a wide moat; few houses are pervaded by such an air of romantic and melancholy decay. A few miles away is the more famous Château d'O, a Renaissance building for the most part, crowned with a fantastic cluster of tall conical roofs; while for those who have a taste for the classical, there is Bourg-St-Léonard, which is thought to have been designed by J. A. Gabriel, and is approached through a splendid formal garden. There are also many others.

In this district is the National Stud at Le Pin, which was founded by Louis XIV. It is laid out on a magnificent scale, with long glades of approach leading to a vast forecourt; at the far end of this lies a seventeenth-century château, now used as offices, raised on a terrace from which there is a wide view over the valley of the Euse.   On either side of the court are the stables containing several hundred stallions of breeds varying from huge grey *percherons,* through the several classes of farm and army horse, to polo ponies and trotters.   Perhaps owing to their size the *percherons* seem to predominate, so that after a tour of the stables one carries away an impression of endless avenues of majestic dappled rumps.

In the inner corner of the great right angle of coastline which is formed by the junction of Normandy and Brittany lies Mont St. Michel, the famous fortified abbey which was one of the few strongholds on this coast which the English were never able to capture. Its position is very remarkable: the great rock on which the buildings stand rises abruptly a few kilometres from the shore, to which it is joined by a causeway.   At high tide it is completely surrounded by water, but at low the sea retires swiftly to a distance of seven or eight miles, leaving the Mount high and dry in a waste of dangerous quicksands.   The abbey church stands on the summit of the rock and is approached from the gateway in the walls round the base by cobbled ramps, half streets, half steps, which pass through the group of houses which clings to the steep slopes.   In this little town is the restaurant founded in the last century by Mère Poulard, whose omelettes were the most famous in France.

The greater part of the abbey church was built about the middle of the eleventh century, and is a splendidly robust example of Romanesque architecture; the choir, however, dates from three hundred years later, and with its *flamboyant,* decoration of pinnacles and flying buttresses provides a graceful crown to the majestic outline of rock and buildings.

The small province of Maine lies south of Normandy and corresponds roughly to the departments of Sarthe and Mayenne.   After early years of independence, it was united in 1110 to Anjou, and thus passed to the English crown when Henry Plantagenet, who was born at Le Mans, the capital, became King of England.   It was lost by John, with the greater part of his possessions, and has remained a part of France ever since, save for a brief period of twenty-three years during the Hundred Years War, when it was recaptured once more by the English.

It is an agreeable agricultural district of small arable fields, amongst which are set prosperous-looking homesteads, consisting of cottages and large stone barns surrounded by massive, well-built, circular stacks of golden straw.   All about the fields are apple-trees, which also line the

28   Bayeux Cathedral: the West Front

29   A Normandy Harvest Field

30   A Normandy Cottage

31   A Normandy Farmyard

An Old
Building in
Beauvais

33   Shipping at Fécamp

roads, with here and there on the steeper slopes woods of oak with a mixture of beech and ash; while in the valleys, through which flow little streams, are plantations of poplars. It is all very pretty and domestic.

The villages and market towns are undistinguished, and consist in general of one long straggling street of single-storeyed houses built of rough stone, stucco-faced and cream-washed. The colour is not unattractive, but as extreme examples of ribbon development they would not appeal to the town-planner.

Through this pleasant countryside one approaches Le Mans, which lies in the wide valley of the Sarthe. It is a large, busy town, with long wide streets and many squares which are usually congested with animated markets. For the most part it is modern and uninteresting, but it is given a certain picturesqueness by the slopes on which it is built. The cathedral, however, in the north part of the town, standing on a precipitous hill above the Sarthe, is surrounded by streets of very early houses, where stone doorways, carved friezes, and high projecting gables remain little altered since the fifteenth century. One of the handsomest of these buildings is known as the House of Queen Berengaria, but as it cannot have been built until nearly two centuries after her death, the name is somewhat misleading. The queen, who was the wife of Richard Cœur-de-Lion, is buried in the adjacent cathedral beneath an interesting thirteenth-century tomb.

The Romanesque and gothic styles have seldom been more curiously combined than in the cathedral. The original building, which was in the former, was partially destroyed by fire in the twelfth century, and was restored in the latter manner; thus Romanesque pillars support gothic arches, and one style mingles with the other, sometimes successfully, but at others with rather grotesque results. The stained glass in the choir, which dates from the thirteenth and fourteenth centuries, is exceedingly beautiful.

The only other town of any considerable size in Maine is Laval, which is now the capital of the department of Mayenne. A long wide street passes straight through the centre, descending a long slope to the bridge over the river Mayenne and rising again on the far side. On high ground near the river stands the very majestic castle, which presents a fine appearance from the town, but is not of great interest on closer inspection. It is now used as law courts.

East of the province of Maine lies the great triangle of Brittany, its blunt point of Finistère, a pendant to the other Finisterre nearly five hundred miles away across the rough waters of the Bay of Biscay, being the apex, and the almost straight north and south line bordered by

Normandy, Maine, Anjou, Poitou the base. It is a district one inevitably associates with a hard countryside, a fierce rocky coastline, elaborate stone calvaries, tough peasants in traditional dress, and rugged stone cottages filled with carved cupboards and brass and copper pots and pans. This is fortunately a rather exaggerated picture, and, although partly true of the north, is hardly applicable to the comparatively radiant and gentle stretch of country bordering the southern coast.

Owing to its geographical position, the province has always remained curiously isolated from the main body of France, and it is only during the last century, since the building of railways, that it has become more developed and civilised. Although in many ways the Bretons are a religious people, paganism is said to have flourished until the seventeenth century, and then only to have been abolished with difficulty, while even to-day the influence of witches and fairies is not entirely discounted. The latter belief is characteristic of a Celtic people, and here as in the Auvergne, and also in a rather lesser degree in Cornwall, myths and fabulous stories have been kept alive amongst the inhabitants for countless generations.

The capital of a province has usually a close relationship to the district over which it presides; it is in a sense a microcosm of the characteristics of the inhabitants and the local architecture of the country. Rennes, however, is a striking exception to this rule, and few towns could be less representative of the spirit of Brittany. Its foundation on a site near the junction of the rivers Ille and Vilaine dates back to pre-Roman times, and since the tenth century it has been the capital of Brittany. In the course of centuries a fairly extensive town of confused narrow streets grew up which was lacking in all the essential dignity of a town of importance. By good fortune, however, a fire broke out in 1720 which, raging for seven days, entirely destroyed the heart of the town. The city fathers, seizing an opportunity such as had been so disastrously lost by their counterparts in the City of London half a century before, laid out their ravaged capital on a spacious classical plan of fine streets and squares, giving long vistas up and down the gentle slopes on which the town lies. Gabriel was called in to design a new town-hall in one of the main squares, and produced one of the greatest ornaments of the town, a building planned in a wide semicircle, with elaborate end pavilions and a tall, graceful central cupola. The elevations are exceedingly happy both in proportion and in detail, but the fine rooms in the interior were damaged by a less fortunate fire during the last century, and were restored in the civic taste of the 'nineties.

A lucky survival from the fire of 1720 was the Palais de Justice, which was admirably worked into the new lay-out. It was begun in 1618, from designs by Solomon de Brosse, as the seat of the Breton Parliament, and was completed about forty years later. The panelled rooms, now used as law courts, have been remarkably well preserved, and one, panelled in oak, contains what is perhaps the most magnificent carving of this period in France.

The cathedral, which was built at various times between 1787 and 1844, is a startling break with the traditional baroque church architecture of the late-eighteenth century, while the interior has the aspect of a Regency London club rather than a religious building. Rennes stands, indeed, like an exotic and sophisticated interloper amongst the robust towns of Brittany.

It is curious to note Augustus Hare's views on Rennes set forth in 1865: "It has the distinction of being the dullest, as it is almost the ugliest town in France . . . there is nothing whatever worth seeing." Judging by the indifference of the hotels, it must be assumed that foreign tourists are still kept away by Mr. Hare's disparaging remarks.

East of Rennes, near the border of Normandy, lie two interesting mediæval fortified towns, Fougères and Vitré. The former has spread beyond its walls, but the latter is still partially surrounded, and with its great machicolated gateways and vast fourteenth-century castle presents a very formidable appearance. Within the walls lies the curious church of Notre Dame, dating from the sixteenth century; with its many pinnacles and decorated gables it has all the gaiety of Strawberry Hill gothic.

Northwards is Dinan, also strongly fortified in an almost impregnable position above the Rance, and on a rocky peninsula where the river estuary opens to the sea is St. Malo. The massive ramparts and towers, which were built as a protection principally against the English, but also in part against the French, from whom the town retained its independence for a considerable time, still rise from the granite rocks which are washed by the sea at high tide. The fortifications reach a crescendo of strength in the pentagonal castle built by Duke François II during the fifteenth century at the north-west corner, where a narrow isthmus connects the town with the mainland. Within the walls there is agreeable architecture of all ages, including several streets of good eighteenth-century houses, the seemly classical façades of which, rising above the mediæval walls, make a charming but incongruous picture. On a little island of rocks which rises from the sea a short way from the shore, known as the Grand Bé, is the tomb of Chateaubriand, who was here buried in a grave hewn in the solid stone in 1848.

The great stretch of plain which takes up the eastern end of Brittany has something of the character of Normandy, with small grass fields, apple-trees, and poplars. The latter are, in this part, tonsured of all branches except for a small tuft at the top—a system which may be a successful means of increasing the timber growth, but is devastating to the aspect of the countryside. Westward, the country rises to a central plateau of deserted stony moorland, strongly reminiscent of the bleaker parts of Yorkshire or Scotland. Until late years this great stretch of country was entirely unproductive, but parts of it have now been cleared and converted into pasture; it remains, however, thin, poor land, and it requires a perpetual struggle to keep the fields free from the destructive inroads of bracken, gorse, and heather.

When Arthur Young, the democratic agriculturalist, visited Brittany in 1788, he was horrified by the derelict appearance of the country. "One third of what I have seen of this province"; he wrote, "seems uncultivated, and nearly all of it is misery"; and he goes on to describe the peasants' houses as "miserable heaps of dirt."

On the lower ground near the coast, where the soil is deeper, market-gardening is carried on with some success, and vegetables are sent to the port of St. Malo for despatch to the English market. Unfortunately not only the soil but also the climate is uncongenial to agriculture; cold fogs sweep in from the sea, and gales blowing from the north and west tear across the peninsula, so that trees are distorted and spring foliage is withered before it has fully opened.

It is strange that this country should produce a race which is undoubtedly the handsomest in France. One sees, however, little except youth and old age, and it seems that the battle against nature soon dissipates young charms.

The towns and villages along the northern coast, such as St. Brieuc, are as stern and hard as the countryside. The houses are built of rough blocks of brown ironstone with dressings of unyielding grey granite and roofs of slate; the gardens contain few flowers to brighten the sad picture. The more easterly Breton villages all centre round a large modern church built in the second half of the last century; they are a tribute to the piety but not to the architectural taste of their builders. Further west, in the department of Finistère, the villages become rather gayer and more picturesque, and some contain fine churches, such as Plabennec and Le Folgoët. The latter has a particularly splendid specimen dating from the fifteenth century, which rises surprisingly amidst the modest cluster of colour-washed cottages which comprises the village. For five centuries it has been a place of pilgrimage following the death of an idiot boy from whose grave grew a lily on the

34 The Black Cliffs of Brittany: Pointe du Raz

35 Brittany: a Road beside the Sea

36   The Towers of Quimper,
        Brittany

37   A Country Church in Brittany:
        Le Folgoët

pistils of which were written in letters of gold the words "O Maria." The church now covers the site of this startling occurrence.

The capital of Finistère, Brest, which is one of the most important naval ports of France, is an agreeable, jolly town, but contains little of architectural interest. Its position is charming, on the shores of the Rade de Brest, a wide indented bay which stretches far inland and has only a small opening to the sea. Long straight streets stretch through the town and descend to the dockyard, in which is kept, amongst many objects which are hidden from foreign eyes, the "Carnot de l'Empereur," a state barge built for Napoleon in 1810. It is conceived with all that riot of invention which invariably inspires designers of coaches and barges: dolphins, fish, flowers, leaves are employed with a lavish but entirely successful abandon, while above the cabin golden cherubs stagger under the weight of a mammoth Imperial Crown. The castle on the cliffs facing the open sea and the remains of Vauban's fortifications, which were constructed soon after Richelieu turned the town into a naval port, are perhaps the only other "sights."

A few miles from Brest, France reaches its most westerly point in the little windswept town of Le Conquet, and a short way south is the important lighthouse of St. Mathieu, the svelte black-and-white body of which emerges incongruously from the ruins of a Benedictine abbey. As early as the sixth century a monastery was founded in this position, exposed to every gale and storm, above the vicious black cliffs which show a geological link with Cornwall, but the great church, which was reduced to its present state at the Revolution, dates from the thirteenth century.

South of Brest, Brittany adopts a gentler aspect, and to the inhabitants at least it appears to possess the same relation to the north as does Provence to Picardy. To the visitor the change seems less sensational, but there is no doubt that although the vegetation remains substantially the same, the country loses its rough, windswept look. Trees are larger, and fields more open, the earth is less stony, and fruit-trees reappear; gorse and bracken still stifle an occasional field, but more rarely than in the north.

The southern side of the Rade de Brest is formed by the peninsula of de Crozon, on which are many little seaside resorts facing the Bay of Douarnenez. In this remote district the Breton costume is worn more universally than anywhere else in the province; almost every woman is attired in the stiff white linen cap and dark frock, and many of the men wear the round black hats and brown suits of this becoming get-up.

The principal town of southern Finistère is Quimper, which lies on the banks of the little river Odet, the wide estuary of which makes it into a modest port.   The main street, shaded by tall planes, passes along the east bank of the river, and on the further side rises a steep hill thickly covered with beech-trees.   This close union of town and wood is unusual and attractive.   Some of the streets are bordered by picturesque timbered houses with high overhanging gables dating from the fifteenth and sixteenth centuries;   there are also several imposing examples of the seventeenth century.   The cathedral is a large gothic building, begun in the thirteenth and completed in the sixteenth century;   in spite of considerable architectural merit, it has a curiously unsympathetic air which may perhaps be due to excessive restoration. The fact that the nave and the choir are built on a slightly different axis adds to the feeling of discomfort.

The flat stretch of country which borders the southern coast of Brittany is somewhat reminiscent of the bleaker parts of Provence, but it lacks the redeeming undulations.   The soil is stony and poor, with frequent outcrops of rock, and supports little in the way of vegetation; only the unexacting pine-tree seems to flourish.   Amongst these rather sad plains, in the department of Morbihan near the little town of Carnac, stands the group of stones which is said to be the most remarkable megalithic remains in the world.   Great grey monoliths are placed in eleven rows to form long avenues which march across the countryside; at the beginning ten to twelve feet in height, they reduce where the lines end to three or four feet.   There are several groups of these alignments in the neighbourhood, and since the rows point one to the other it is conjectured that they may at one time have been connected. Their exact significance still remains undecided, although theory and counter-theory have been animatedly advanced for the last century or more.

The capital of Morbihan, Vannes, lies a few miles east of Carnac, close to a curious stretch of indented marshy coast which borders the Bay of Quiberon.   The ramparts which originally surrounded the town survive in part and are pierced by several fine gateways, but since building has spread the original form has been lost.   Twisting streets of extraordinary narrowness still surround the cathedral, but nearby one or two handsome squares were formed early in the last century which lessen the mediæval aspect.   In the left transept of the cathedral is the tomb of St. Vincent Ferrier, the draconian Dominican, who died in 1419.

On the promontory between the mouth of the Vilaine, Brittany's largest river, and the vast estuary of the Loire are some of the most popular seaside towns on this coast.   Of these, La Baule is the most attractive; it has a superb position on a wide shallow bay facing due south, with miles of sandy beach stretching between low projecting points of cliff and a thick belt of pinewoods to protect the shore from north winds. Nature, indeed, has lavished its amenities, and it has been left to man to mar the picture by hideous development during the last twenty years.

Inland from La Baule is the little mediæval town of Guérande, which still retains its walls intact; all modern building has been banished beyond a wide boulevard, so that the ramparts and the great Porte St. Michel, half castle, half gatehouse, still appear as impressive as when they were built five centuries ago.

At the mouth of the Loire, which at this point is nearly two miles wide, is St. Nazaire, a rather dreary town given up to shipbuilding, but with a popular summer beach on its western side. From St. Nazaire to Nantes the Loire flows through country which has lost all trace of the harsh Breton landscape, although it is still within the borders of Brittany. In the valley on either side of the river are fertile stretches of soil in which are grown vegetables, maize, roots, cabbages, and so forth, as well as an occasional patch of vines which produce the excellent local wine, Muscadet. Beyond this valley the ground rises to shallow rolling hills covered with arable fields and large sweeps of woods, amongst which are set a considerable number of châteaux, some surrounded by fine parks. In this lovely countryside lies the historic city of Nantes, which now, owing to industrial development, is the seventh largest town in France. It is conveniently divided into three parts, the mediæval, the eighteenth-century, and the commercial; the two former contain several buildings of interest. The castle stands close to the docks, which have been formed from a branch of the Loire, and was originally surrounded by a moat fed by the waters of the river; now the hexagon of curtain-wall and robust towers rises from a well-kept sward. Part of the exterior walls dates back to the tenth century, but their present appearance is principally due to Francis II, Duke of Brittany, who rebuilt the castle from the designs of Mathelin Rodier in 1466. Within the courtyard are several imposing towers built in the early Renaissance style and covered with the mixture of gothic and classical ornamentation which was popular at that period. In the northern corner of the court is a tower dating from the twelfth century; within its massive walls was incarcerated Gilles de Rais, the infamous "Bluebeard," who here received his ultimate reward from the executioner in 1440.

Close to the castle stands the high, graceful cathedral of St. Pierre, also designed by Rodier, who was clearly a versatile and accomplished artist. Although begun in 1434, when Duke Jean V laid the first stone, building continued until the middle of the seventeenth and was not finally completed until the nineteenth century. It is surprising that a cathedral built over so long a span and during years of such doubtful gothic taste should be so successful. In the south transept stands the magnificent tomb of Duke Francis II, who died in 1488, with his second wife, Marguerite de Foix, which was moved to the cathedral in 1817 from its original place in the Carmelite church. It was rifled and damaged during the Revolution, and the remains of Marguerite of Brittany, the duke's first wife, and the heart of their daughter and heiress, Anne, which were immured in the same tomb, have disappeared. Close to the cathedral is the handsome Place Maréchal Foch, which, unlike most of this quarter, is purely eighteenth-century in character; but eastward stretches a maze of narrow streets which still contain a large number of picturesque early houses.

The eighteenth-century part of the town covers the rising ground beyond the little river Erdre, which flows southward into the docks and so by the Canal St. Felix into a branch of the Loire. The centre of the district is the Place Graslin, from which the streets radiate on a formal plan. The upper side of this apse-ended square is filled by the handsome Corinthian portico of the theatre, which was built in 1788 and is reminiscent of the larger building designed by Victor Louis in Bordeaux; the interior has unfortunately been considerably altered. On the lower side, contained within the curve of the simple classical façade, is a café-restaurant, the decoration of which will delight any enthusiast for the "Art Nouveau" style. There is no more interesting example in the country.

Nantes will always be famous for the edict by which, in 1598, Henri IV, following thirty-five years of civil war, gave religious liberty to the Protestants; this tolerant measure was revoked eighty-seven years later by Louis XIV.

Perhaps the most romantic incident in the history of Nantes came during the nineteenth century, when, following the flight of Charles X, his daughter-in-law, the Duchesse de Berry, endeavoured to stimulate a movement amongst the loyal people of the Vendée in favour of her son, the Comte de Chambord, in opposition to the claims of Louis-Philippe of Orléans. She met with little success, and after great personal privations was compelled to take refuge in the house of a friend, at No. 3 rue Haute-du-Château in Nantes. Here, concealed in a small space formed in a chimney to which the only entrance was through an iron door in the back of the hearth, she was able to elude an intensive house-to-house search. Her whereabouts were eventually

A Breton Calvary:
Plougouven

39 A Breton Village Church:
Plabennec

40   ''La Dévote''

disclosed to the military, but still no trace of her was discovered until the guards in the house, feeling cold, lit a fire in the grate, when the duchess and her three companions, covered with soot and dust, were compelled to make a rather undignified appearance on all fours. They were imprisoned for a time in the castle, but were soon after freed and expelled from the country.

CHAPTER III

ALSACE-LORRAINE AND THE NORTHERN PLAINS

EMBRACING the broad trough of the Rhine between the Vosges and the Black Forest, Alsace and Lorraine stretch from Belfort in the south to the frontier of Luxembourg. To-day they are divided into the three departments: Haut-Rhin, Bas-Rhin, and Moselle, while since 1871 Belfort has been the capital of its own little territorial division, called the "Trouée de Belfort." Taken as a whole, Alsace-Lorraine is a region of great scenic and artistic interest, while the fact that it is a border country, occupied in turn by the Gallic and Teutonic races, endows it with a charm of subtle contrast denied to countries with less mingled blood.

Belfort, the most southerly town in the ancient province of Alsace, has endured, in harmony with its name, a number of sieges, of which the most memorable were one during the Thirty Years War, a second after the Battle of Leipzig in 1813, and the last and most famous in the winter of 1870, when Colonel Denfert-Rochereau held out for a hundred and three days against the Prussians, and then was allowed to evacuate the town with all the so-called honours of war. These courageous actions are commemorated in the Place de la République by the "Monument des Trois Sièges"—an erection, however, of more humorous than artistic merit.

Although Belfort is rather despised by the average guidebook and its modern quarters can safely be ignored, the old town possesses in the Place d'Armes one of the most charming squares in north-eastern France. Most of the houses date from the seventeenth century, and are built in the colourful *grès rouge*, or red sandstone, which is a feature of the province. The little Hôtel de Ville has a most jaunty air, while the Church of St. Christophe opposite presents, in contrast, a severe neo-classical façade. The middle of the square is occupied by a monument erected in 1884 to the memory of Belfort's last siege. It is aptly called "Quand-Même," and the profiles of Colonel Denfert-Rochereau and Monsieur Thiers appropriately adorn its bleak surface.

Contiguous to the old town lies the romantic Porte de Brisach, the entrance to the ramparts built by Vauban. The interior portico, with its wide pediment, and the simple but elegant columns which support

41 (*opposite*)
Ribeauvillé: an old wine town in Alsace

42 The Lake of Retourneur in the Vosges

43 Muhlbach : a Foothill Village of the Vosges

it are a happy example of the blending of domestic and defensive architecture during the reign of Louis XIV.   Far more spectacular, however,
is the famous "Lion de Belfort" at the foot of the citadel, south of the
ramparts.   This truly magnificent beast, carved by Bartholdi in red
sandstone during the 'seventies, commemorates the siege of 1870.
The lion, which is over seventy-two feet long, stands out strongly from
the sombre rock-face below the citadel.   It is interesting and appropriate to recollect that the sculptor, Bartholdi, was also responsible for
the statue of Liberty in New York harbour.

The road from Belfort to Colmar passes through fertile and wooded
country, and in the "Trouée de Belfort" through a stretch of land
separating the Juras from the foothills of the Vosges.   Ruffach and
Guebwiller are two typical little Alsatian towns with gabled roofs and
quiet squares redolent of cleanliness and prosperity.   The former was
the birthplace of Marshal Lefèbvre, the miller's son who became the
Duke of Danzig, and whose wife was the original of Sardou's "Madame
Sans-Gêne."   Guebwiller, a similar small town, which is notable for
the fine Church of St. Leger in the Rhenish-Romanesque style, lies in
the proximity of the Ballon de Guebwiller, the highest mountain in the
Vosges.   From its summit a splendid view of the Black Forest and the
Alsatian plain can be enjoyed, and in clear weather the Juras and even
the Alps are visible.

Guebwiller lies on the southern extremity of the famous Rhenish
vineyards, which stretch north as far as Kronenburg.   Amongst the
best-known names of their delicious wines, which approximate both
in taste and bouquet to their sister grapes on the other side of the
Rhine, are Mittelwihr, Ribeauvillé, Riquewihr, Chatenois, Dambach,
Rosheim, and Molsheim.   Hops and tobacco are also grown on the
Alsatian plain, and a potash industry is being rapidly developed within
the triangle formed by Thann, Colmar, and Mulhouse.

Beyond Guebwiller, together with the appearance of flourishing
vineyards, the foothills of the Vosges approach nearer to the road.
Two deviations can, however, be made: one east to Neuf-Brisach and
the second west to Gérardmer.   The former is a delightful seventeenth-
century fortress town, built by Vauban in a symmetrical manner in
order to guard the left bank of the Rhine.   Gérardmer, which
traditionally derives its name from Gérard, the first Duke of Lorraine, in
the eleventh century, is a picturesque town situated on a lake in the
heart of the Hautes-Vosges.   The fine linen of the district is made here,
as also the delicious cheeses called *geromés*.   It claims to be visited by a
hundred thousand people a year.

Colmar, the capital of Upper Alsace, is now the chief town in the

6

department of the Haut-Rhin, and it is situated on the river Lauch at the foot of the Vosges. Although the sympathies of its inhabitants during the last century were strongly pro-French, the German tongue is more prevalent in Colmar than in any other town of Alsace and Lorraine. Despite its hideous suburbs and the rude trespass of modern erections in its oldest thoroughfares, Colmar is still a representative Alsatian town, with its narrow and irregular streets and many timbered or painted houses. Of the latter, the Maison Pfister and the Maison des Têtes are renowned for their ornate and fanciful façades. Fortunately, both would be difficult to copy by the architect of a modern road-house.

The great glory of Colmar is, of course, the Musée Unterlinden, which contains a superb collection of the German Primitive school. Of several pictures by the fifteenth-century Martin Schongauer, "La Vierge au Buisson de Roses" is one of the most sensitive and spiritual works of that brilliant master. Mathias Grünewald, whose greatest pictures date from the early sixteenth century, is first represented by his famous Crucifixion, in which the figures at the foot of the Cross are painted with such subtle poignancy. His Nativity delicately portrays the joy of the young mother; while his conversation-piece of Sts. Paul and Anthony Abbot in the desert radiates an atmosphere of spiritual serenity hard to excel. The holy men have a desert background of rocks and palms, while above them, on a desiccated tree, the audacious raven, with a loaf in its mouth, prepares to interrupt the pious intercourse.

The road from Colmar to Strasbourg lies through a flat fertile plain with the magnificent barrier of the Vosges on the left. Shortly before Sélestat on the Ill, the department of Bas-Rhin is reached. Sélestat is one of the most ancient towns in Alsace, and, with its ramshackle houses and narrow, crooked streets, can satisfy the most eager appetite for the picturesque. The Church of Ste. Foy, one of the finest Romanesque buildings in the province, has an unusual if heavy interior, with great arcades supported by thick round columns with cubical capitals. The villages in this neighbourhood are particularly attractive owing to their steep-roofed and half-timbered houses, often huddled together within ramparts entered by a mediæval gateway and protected by a single defensive tower. The villages of Turckheim, Obernai, and Barr are delightful examples of this haphazard grouping, while between the two latter towns, at the Convent of Ste. Odile, the best view of the plain of Alsace can be obtained. From the wooded spur occupied by the convent buildings it is said that three hundred villages can be counted below, while the spire of Strasbourg cathedral is unmistakable in the far distance and the heights of the Black Forest appear like a pale-grey mist on the horizon beyond the Rhine.

The large farmsteads in the neighbourhood of Ste. Odile, which lie near the road, are very noticeable. They are massive half-timbered erections, with the house and barns in a continuous three-sided range. The fourth is pierced by a wicket-gate and encloses the farmyard. When these buildings are grouped together in a village, a large and ornate gothic church of the last century usually towers above it—a monument of piety rather than of good taste. Storks can often be seen on the farmhouses, perched on an iron nest-frame thoughtfully provided by the kindly owners. Geispolsheim is a good example of these farming villages, with their sturdy buildings grouped together for practical and social convenience. The ladies of Geispolsheim are also worthy of attention, since on Sundays they still wear the traditional costume of the parti-coloured bodice and full skirt with the white lace apron.

Strasbourg, the ancient capital of Alsace and now that of the modern department of the Bas-Rhin, is one of the most attractive cities in France. The old town is entirely surrounded by water formed by the Ill on the south-east and south-west sides, while a canalised branch of the same river protects the northern approaches to the city. Strasbourg has had a chequered history, inevitable owing to its geographical locality on the frontier of the Gallic and Teutonic races, and the natural desire of each to dominate such an important strategical position. It was from the fourteenth to the seventeenth centuries, when Strasbourg was independent and under the democratic rule of the Guilds, that the city enjoyed its longest period of peace and prosperity. Unfortunately, this happy state of affairs came to an end in 1681, when Louis XIV incorporated it into France, although he allowed the inhabitants to retain many of their ancient privileges. These were abolished in the early years of the Revolution. It is interesting to recollect that at Strasbourg, in 1792, Rouget de Lisle composed the exhilarating melody of the "Marseillaise" for the army of the Rhine, and that here in 1836 Louis-Napoléon, later Emperor of the French, made his first luckless attempt to regain his uncle's throne. The later history of the place is too well known to require recapitulation, but it must be remembered that, although the city is French once more and strongly Gallic in sympathy, the German tongue is still the more widely spoken. Since, however, the sensible adjustments regarding the Catholic Church made by the French Government some twenty years ago, the great majority of the Strasbourgeois have rejoiced in their liberation from German rule, and there is little disposition on their part to-day to be assimilated into the Third Reich.

Lying to the south-east of the island on which the old city of Strasbourg is situated rises the superb gothic pile of the cathedral, more usually known as the "Münster," of Notre Dame.   Built in red sandstone towards the close of the thirteenth century, the western façade, enriched by innumerable statues and covered with a veil of the most exquisite tracery, rises gracefully to the great height of two hundred and sixteen feet.   Erwin of Steinbach is said to have been the architect, and, in the original plan, had provided for twin towers of equal height rising from the second storey.   Unfortunately these were not completed, and the two unfinished towers were joined by the existing platform on the third storey, above which was raised the northern tower. The elegant spire was erected in the fifteenth century upon the octagonal body of this tower, and it rises to the dizzy height of four hundred and sixty-four feet.   In order to ascend it strong legs are clearly necessary and also a strong head, owing to the alarming apertures in the stonework of the spire.

The interior of the cathedral has been over-restored, and, despite some beautiful glass, the nave seems to lack proportion owing to its great width in comparison with the height; while the choir, although surrounded by an octagonal apse of massive proportions, is defaced by weak frescoes in the Byzantine manner perpetrated in the middle of the last century.   The object of the greatest ornamental beauty in the building, apart from the stained glass, is the *Pilier des Anges*, a thirteenth-century column adorned with ethereal and trumpeting angels.   Nearby is the astronomical clock, a garish and amorphous structure of the sixteenth century, which always attracts a great host of tourists to witness its antics, particularly at noon.   Besides showing the calendar, the position of the planets, and the courses of the sun and moon, at midday the Apostles emerge from its garnished face and bow to the figure of Christ, while a cock with beating wings crows thrice.

Close to the south façade of the cathedral lies the Palais Rohan on the bank of the river Ill.   It is a magnificent classical building erected about 1730 by the architect Robert de Cotte for Armand Gaston de Rohan, the Prince-Archbishop of Strasbourg.   Cotte, who also constructed the dome of the Invalides, was nearly seventy-five when he designed this archiepiscopal palace, and few architects can have planned a more beautiful structure at such an advanced age.   It is, indeed, a great experience to stand in the rectangular court and, after enjoying the severe lines of Cotte's masterpiece, to gaze above the simple arcaded entrance upon the pink lacework spire of the cathedral.   The south front on the Ill is not so happily designed, as the centre pediment is too mean in conception for the great bulk of the wings on either side.

The palace now houses the Musée des Beaux Arts, but, despite the

44   The Roofs of Strasbourg from the Cathedral Tower

45   Old Houses in Strasbourg

46 Riquewihr: looking across the Rooftops to the Vineyards

47 Kaiserberg: the Castle from the Town

48 A Peasant Dance in Alsace

49   A Country Road in Moselle

quality of some of the pictures, the great interest of the interior lies in the superb suite of rooms facing south which were the principal apartments of the Cardinal de Rohan and his successors until 1790, when the palace was seized by the State. The greater part of the interior decorations were carried out by Jean-Auguste Nahl, and the beauty of the painted *boiseries* could not be surpassed even in that period of the most refined taste. The bedroom used by Marie Antoinette on her first arrival in France is a lovely example of rococo art. It is interesting to note that Nahl was born in Berlin, and that most of his work was done either there or in Cassel. In consequence, in the Palais Rohan the decoration approximates more closely to German rococo than to the early Louis XV style.

In the same picturesque vicinity, and in amusing contrast to the severe lines of the archiepiscopal palace, rise a variety of strange old houses dating from the fourteenth to the sixteenth centuries. Typical of Strasbourg, their steeply sloping and tiled roofs often contain as many as three storeys of dormer windows. Of these the best-known are the Maison de l'Œuvre de Notre Dame, half gothic and half Renaissance in architecture, and the Hôtel du Corbeau, encrusted with a multitude of carved masks. This inn, having lodged and fed Turenne in the middle of the seventeenth century and Frederick the Great a hundred years later, is still engaged in the art of hospitality.

It is perhaps rather a relief to abandon this ancient and picturesque vicinity to find a contrast in the Place Kléber, the social centre of the city, where the trams circulate in an endless shrieking procession and the thronged cafés and restaurants provide that wide choice of diversion so typical of France. The middle of the square is occupied by the statue of General Kléber, and his remains are buried below. This Napoleonic officer was stabbed to death at Cairo in 1800 by a crazy Mussulman. Not far from the Kléber rises the thirteenth-century church of St. Thomas, with Romanesque and gothic towers. It should certainly be inspected by the discerning visitor, since, apart from some admirable stained glass, it contains one of the most theatrical and amusing tombs in northern France. Erected in 1777 by the sculptor Pigalle in memory of the Maréchal de Saxe, it portrays the latter descending the steps of a grey marble pyramid towards an open coffin below. On one side "France" tries vainly to hinder his further progress, and on the other Hercules discreetly mourns his earthly rival.

Immediately to the west of Alsace lies Lorraine, which is now divided into the two modern departments of Meurthe-et-Moselle and Moselle. The road from Strasbourg to Nancy, the chief town in the former department, passes through the most delightful undulating country dotted with prosperous farms and variegated by high slopes covered with the vineyards of Kronenburg. This country is indeed a great gastronomic centre, and the kindly tourist when negotiating his car through the frequent gaggles of indignant geese may wonder if the method of "stall-fattening" and "cramming" these amiable birds, in order to enlarge their livers unnaturally, is really humane. Nevertheless, he will probably forget his qualms later when consuming the world-famous *pâtés de foie gras Strasbourgeois.*

Nancy, the old capital of Lorraine, lies in the broad valley of the Meurthe at the foot of wooded hills, and consists of the old town on the north-west and the beautiful "new" town, built on a rectangular plan during the seventeenth and eighteenth centuries. Nancy was the capital of the Dukes of Lorraine since the twelfth century, but it was Stanislas Leczinski, the ex-King of Poland and the father-in-law of Louis XV, who was responsible for its main embellishments. Stanislas received the duchy to console him for the loss of Poland, and, on his death in 1766, Lorraine was incorporated in France.

This duke was responsible for the erection of the Place Stanislas, one of the most beautiful squares built in Europe during the eighteenth century. The architect was Héré, who also constructed various country houses, including Bazeilles, his masterpiece, near Sedan. The Place Stanislas is enclosed by buildings of uniform design, of which the largest is the Hôtel de Ville, while the theatre and the Grand Hotel stand side by side on the north-easterly edge of the square. These latter buildings, in their fine proportions and dignified unity, might serve as models of civic architecture in any age. At the north-east and north-west angles of the square rise two monumental fountains with leaden statues backed by wrought-iron gilded railings. These and the delicate screens of ironwork were designed by the native artist Jean Lamour, and are masterpieces of the metalworker's art of the eighteenth century. It is indeed difficult to leave the Place Stanislas, where Héré and Lamour have lavished their genius on a creation of such theatrical yet finished beauty.

A short distance up the rue Héré, and opposite the Hôtel de Ville, lies the triumphal arch built by that architect in honour of a visit from Louis XV. It has noble yet conventional proportions. Behind it lies the Palais du Gouvernement, with its long, simple classical façade and arcade with Ionic columns. Adjoining this building is the over-restored and hideous Palais Ducal, now used for the Musée Lorraine, in which is housed a confused and rather ordinary collection of local art.

Nancy is not very rich in ecclesiastical architecture. The cathedral has a topheavy classical façade leading to an interior of little interest considering that it was planned by Mansard.   Eight chapels, however, are approached by pretty iron grilles by Lamour and his colleague, Jean Maire.   More interesting is the Chapelle de Bonsecours, built by the great Héré in 1738.   The exterior is ornamented with a screen of Corinthian columns above which rises a pretty classical clock-tower, shaped like a small rectangular box.   The simple aisleless interior contains the tombs of Duke Stanislas and his wife, with statues by Lambert Adam.   The former has the theatrical charm of the baroque, with Stanislas's semi-recumbent figure apparently on the point of assuming a vertical position, while below him stands a half-draped globe with appropriate figures abandoned to grief.

The road from Nancy north to Metz lies through the windswept plain of the Moselle, but the bibulous will enjoy the great expanses of hops which provide the French people with a large proportion of their beer. Pears, yellow plums, pigs, and macaroons are also specialities of the vicinity, but industrial Lorraine is not a province of particular interest to the average visitor.   Metz, however, the former capital of German Lorraine, and now the chief town in the department of the Moselle, is a place of considerable charm with important historical connections. Dominated for a time in the Dark Ages by Henry the Fowler, that spirited baritone of *Lohengrin*, Metz became a free town in the twelfth century and retained its liberty until the Wars of Religion, when it was incorporated in France.   It withstood two sieges during the Napoleonic period, and preserved its sobriquet of "La Pucelle" until 1870, when Marshal Bazaine ignominiously surrendered to the Prussians.   Marshal Pétain had the satisfaction of effacing this humiliation when he occupied Metz on November 19th, 1918.   Rabelais was the town physician of Metz in the middle of the sixteenth century, and Ambroise Thomas, the composer of *Mignon*, was born there in 1811.   Paul Verlaine was a rather incongruous native of this stalwart fortified town.

The traveller who arrives at Metz by train will find himself in one of the most hideous and grandiose stations in Europe.   It was built under the Germans in 1908 in what was supposed to be the Romanesque style.   Grey sandstone was used, and this fantastic erection was capped by a spinach-green roof.   It should, however, be preserved, since, before long, it will probably be admired.   The streets in the neighbourhood of the station are said to have been designed by the Emperor William II, but they hardly do credit to that monarch's active and erudite brain.   In pleasant contrast to these flamboyant thoroughfares are the narrow and picturesque streets in the old French quarter, near the cathedral, where the town is divided into several islands linked together by bridges and formed by the confluence of the

Seille and the Moselle.   The cathedral itself is a late-gothic erection mainly built by the architect Pierre Perrat, who died in 1440.   It is characterised by its great height and the unusual development of window space.   The interior contains few objects of outstanding interest, with the exception, in the north aisle, of an immense and beautiful porphyry basin, said to be of Roman origin and once used as a font.   The exterior, however, is beautified by a wealth of flying buttresses and the Tour de la Mutte, with its elegant openwork spire. The portal of the western façade is flanked by statues of the Prophets, amongst whom Daniel is portrayed, with some lack of humour, with the martial features of William II.   When Metz was retaken by the French in 1918 this figure was pertinently if tastelessly inscribed with the words "Sic transit gloria mundi."

The road from Metz to Verdun is of little scenic interest, although some claret grapes grow near Gravelotte, famous for the courageous but vain charge of the French cavalry in the 1870 war, while the river Orne, which is reached at Conflans-Jarny, is renowned for its abundance of crayfish.   Verdun, in the department of the Meuse, is still over-shadowed by the tragic part it played in the last war, and its monuments are inconsiderable apart from their military interest.   It should, how-ever, be remembered, particularly by those incredulous of the futility of war, that during Falkenhayn's great offensive against Verdun in February, 1916, three hundred thousand Germans were killed, and it is probable that, during the successful defence of the fortress under Pétain and Nivelle, an equal number of French soldiers perished.

Verdun, which is situated in the north of the department of the Meuse, is separated from the southern portion by the Meuse itself and the river Aire.   This is a bleak part of France.   Further south, in more hilly and wooded country, lies Bar-le-Duc, the chief town of the department and once the home of the Old Pretender, whence he made his unsuccessful descent upon Scotland in 1715.   Much of the town is now industrialised, but south-east of the river Ornain, which bisects it, lies the original, quiet old town with many houses dating from the fifteenth to the seventeenth centuries.   The Church of St. Pierre dominates this quarter, and in this rather ordinary late-gothic erection can be seen a most macabre monument.   It is the tomb of René de Chalon, Prince of Orange, who died in 1544, surmounted by the most realistic sculptured "cadaver" of the human body in decay.

Ligny-en-Barrois, to the east of Bar-le-Duc, is a fascinating little town of a remarkable architectural homogeneity, with eighteenth-century streets reminiscent of those on the outskirts of Versailles. The road thence, returning through Bar-le-Duc to Châlons-sur-Marne,

50 (opposite)
A Fountain in the Place Stanislas, Nancy

51 Nancy: the Old Palace, with a foreground of Lamour's Ironwork

passes through the undulating and vine-clad valley of the Ornain. It lies on the eastern extremity of the famous district which produces the champagne wine. The verdant "Barrois," as this region is called, terminates on the fringe of the department of the Marne. Thence the scenery becomes less interesting, particularly on entering the ill-favoured district of the "Champagne Pouilleuse" (i.e. lousy), so called from its barren soil. The well-situated and prettily-named village of Bussy-le-Repos is passed before reaching the Carrefour de la Grande Romaine, with pinewoods on either side and a distant view of Chalons-sur-Marne.

Châlons, which is the chief town of the department of the Marne, might be called from its many military establishments the Aldershot of France. Apart from its cathedral, described in another section, Chalons possesses two noteworthy twelfth-century churches in St. Alpin, which has preserved the main portal and nave of the original plan, and Notre-Dame-en-Vaux, with its elegant spires and interesting stained-glass windows of the sixteenth century. Chalons was once a centre of the wool trade, a fact which was recalled by both Chaucer and Swift. The former refers to the woollen cloth made here as "Chalouns," while the Dean mentions it as "Shalloons." Two events of historical interest have occurred in Châlons. The first was in 1147, when St. Bernard preached the First Crusade in the presence of Pope Eugenius IV and Louis VII. The second happened in 1791, when Louis XVI and his family were lodged in the *préfecture* on their ignominious return from the "flight to Varennes."

The road from Châlons to Rheims through Épernay crosses a typical undulating plain, with a fine view to the south over the valley of the Marne. Shortly after leaving the vicinity of Châlons, the great expanses of the Champagne vineyards are reached, which stretch from the south of Sézanne to Rethel, north of Rheims. Here, of course, grow the grapes which produce the world-famous sparkling wines to which the old province of Champagne has given its name. Épernay is now the chief centre of the champagne trade, and the wines made here are known as the *Vins de la Rivière*, to distinguish them from the *Vins de la Montagne* produced in the neighbourhood of Rheims. The Faubourg de la Folie in Épernay contains the immense premises of the principal wine merchants. Many of these firms show their cellars to visitors, and a tour of one of these labyrinthine galleries of wine is an entrancing experience. The cellars are excavated from the chalky rock on which the town is built, and while sometimes they are vaulted with brick, the majority are hewn directly out of the chalk. Here the juice of the grapes remains for four or five years and, after undergoing various maturing processes, emerges as "champagne." Perhaps the most frequently visited of these cellars are the "Caves Chandon" and the "Caves Mercier"; the latter contain a colossal tun said to hold two hundred thousand bottles of wine, and the walls of the "Cave" are ornamented with sculpture of an appropriate Bacchic nature.

Rheims to-day is rather a melancholy city, since, in rebuilding it after 1918, the inevitable decrease in the population as a result of the war was overlooked. In consequence the trim, bleak streets lack that immense throng so characteristic of French towns, and many of the larger cafés, through lack of sufficient customers, are deprived of that Gallic vitality which English people so naturally and rightly admire. The cathedral itself and the historical connections of Rheims are discussed in another section, but not the Musée des Beaux Arts, which to-day houses the superb collection of tapestries which once adorned the cathedral walls. Of these, the oldest and perhaps the finest were made about 1440 and represent scenes from the life of Clovis. Approximately of the same period are the priceless "Toiles Peintes," painted fabrics inspired by the mystery plays, which served as patterns for the tapestries. The mysteries of the Passion, the Resurrection, and the Last Judgment are works of exquisite beauty.

North of the Marne lies the department of the Ardennes, formerly the northern portion of the province of Champagne, which stretches to the Belgian frontier. Although much of this district has been defaced by industry, the beautiful forest of the Ardennes covers its northern plateau and stretches into Belgium. The wild boar can still be hunted in these spacious woods. Mezières is the chief town of the Ardennes, lying on the left bank of the Meuse. It is an ancient fortified place, but devoid of particular interest to-day. On the opposite side of the Meuse is situated Charleville, largely occupied with the manufacture of hardware and nails; but in the centre of the town lies the delightful Place Ducale, surrounded by arcades under its steep-roofed houses of the seventeenth century. This square was built by the Duke Charles of Gonzaga, after whom Charleville was named. North of Mezières-Charleville the Meuse ascends through the forest of the Ardennes, but the valley is sadly disfigured by ironworks and quarries.

South-east of these towns lies Sedan, next in fame during the last century to Waterloo as a scene of disaster for French arms. It is prettily situated at the foot of wooded hills that rise above the right bank of the Meuse. Although the fortress is now dismantled and there is little of artistic interest in the town, the citadel on the hill to the east incorporates a fifteenth-century château, and it was from here that Napoleon III watched the disastrous progress of the battle on September

1st, 1870. The Hôtel de la Croix d'Or in the Place Turenne is, however, more poignantly associated with Louis-Napoléon, since a tablet by the entrance recalls the fact that the distraught and suffering Emperor slept here during the battle. South of Sedan lies the little village of Donchery, where, in a weaver's cottage, Napoleon was closeted for two hours with the truculent and unshaved Bismarck, in a futile attempt to persuade him to modify his harsh terms of peace. Nearby at Bellevue, in the undistinguished château belonging to Monsieur Armour, the Emperor received the news of the unconditional surrender of his army of eighty-seven thousand men under Marshal MacMahon.

After Mezières-Charleville and Sedan, the two most important towns in the Ardennes are Vouziers and Rethel, both lying on the Aisne—a river which provides for this rather uninteresting countryside a plentiful supply of trout, pike, and crayfish. Rethel, after Mezières, is the best gastronomic centre in the Ardennes, and, besides fish and game *pâtés*, it specialises in *andouillettes*, or small pork sausages, and *boudin blanc*—rather a misleading name for the somewhat alarming contents of a "white pudding."

West of the Ardennes lies the department of the Aisne, which consists of the northern part of the Île-de-France and a western strip of Picardy. Laon, which is the chief town in the department, is splendidly situated on a solitary hill above a featureless plain. The summit of this height is crowned by one of the finest cathedrals in France. Notre Dame, which was begun in 1115, after a fire which had destroyed the previous structure, was completed in 1230, and, despite the efforts of the mid-nineteenth-century restorer, still retains the imprint of its inspired designers. Originally planned to carry seven towers, only four of these elegant constructions are finished, and the single spire above the façade which, judging from eighteenth-century prints, must have possessed exceptional grace, was unfortunately destroyed at the Revolution. The three deeply recessed doors which pierce the entrance-front are cavernous in their depth and obscurity, but in general the façade has been over-restored, and the sculptures of the liberal arts appear self-conscious on a gothic cathedral. More interesting are the gigantic oxen which project from the upper stages of the west tower. Their presence is due to the legend that these pious animals dragged the stone for the cathedral up the steep incline of their own accord.

The interior is remarkable for the wide and luminous nave and for the beautiful grouping of the pillars, from the capitals of which sheaves of columns ascend through the triforium and clerestory to converge in the vault. The unusually deep choir is surrounded by delicate eighteenth-century grilles, but, in place of the usual chevet, terminates abruptly in the English manner in a straight east wall, which is pierced by three lancet windows filled with exquisite stained glass.   Delightful walks can be taken in the precipitous neighbourhood of the cathedral by those with good hearts and legs; the Ruelle Pourrier, with its mediæval houses, is particularly attractive where it branches north to terminate in the massive Porte d'Ardon, an impressive thirteenth-century gateway.

The road from Laon to Soissons passes over a plain of great agricultural value, and here, besides cereals, are grown crops of beans, artichokes, and sugar-beet.   Vailly and Braisne are left on the east, both of which lie on the extreme western edge of the Champagne country. The latter little town possesses the remains of the beautiful Abbey Church of St. Yved, built in the twelfth century and modelled on Laon Cathedral.   Soissons is prettily situated in comparison with most towns in the north of France, since it lies on the left bank of the Aisne in a basin surrounded by wooded hills.   The town was cruelly bombarded during the last war, but, like Rheims, it has made a spectacular recovery. To-day it is the centre of a thriving industry both in corn and in the beans which are called *soissons* after it.   The north side and the nave of the cathedral, which is dedicated to Sts. Gervais and Portais, was completely shattered by German shells, and at the end of the war the western façade stood entirely detached from the remainder of the ruined building.   The choir and the beautiful south transept, with its apsidal termination, fortunately escaped vital injury.   South of Soissons lies the village of Buzancy, where, in a charming inscription on the War Memorial, the martial link between France and Scotland is thus described:

"Ici fleurira le glorieux Chardon d'Écosse parmi les Roses de France."

To the west of the department of the Aisne stretches that of the Somme, which originally formed part of the old province of Picardy. This region has not been particularly blessed by nature, nor respected by man, since war has more than once ravaged its timbered slopes and the wide chalk downs which are dissected by the Somme, the Celle, the Oise, and the Avre.   In the Middle Ages the province was divided into Upper and Lower Picardy.   The former comprised the *pays*, or feudal districts, of Amienois, Santerre, Vermandois, and Thiérache. Lower Picardy consisted of the Pays Réconquis (Calais and its vicinity), the Boulonnais, Ponthieu, with Abbeville and Vimeu.   Picardy is the country of Peter the Hermit, since the great crusader was born at Amiens in the second half of the eleventh century.

The principal interest of Amiens, apart from its immense cathedral,

52 Northern Ploughlands

53   The Place Ducale, Charleville

55   Amiens: Old H⟨

54　Boulogne from the Harbour

ow of the Cathedral

56   A Tree-fringed Road in the Marne

described in another section, is the large number of canals formed from the waters of the Somme, the Celle, and the Avre, which flow through it and lend charm to a town which suffered so cruelly during the last war.   Amiens is connected with two famous treaties: that signed in 1550 between Edward VI and Henri II and the better-known and more ephemeral one concluded in 1802 between Napoleon and England with her continental allies.   The "Mise d'Amiens" in 1264, which can also be regarded as a treaty, consisted of the decision given by St. Louis as arbitrator in the dispute between Henry III and the English barons under Simon de Montfort.   It constituted a rare example of successful mediation in the Middle Ages.

The two most important towns in the Somme, after Amiens, are Abbeville and Montdidier, lying respectively in the north-western and southern parts of the region.   As the capital of Ponthieu the former came to Edward I in 1272 on his marriage with Eleanor of Castille and remained in English hands until 1477.   The Church of St. Vulfran is the only building of interest in the town, and its north front, with three ornate portals, is an outstanding example of the *flamboyant* style. Montdidier is pleasantly situated on a hill above a remarkably dull countryside from the scenic point of view, although on the plains below are produced the special local cheeses called *Les Rollots*, and the *primeurs*, which is a collective name given to early vegetables and fruit. This town was laid in ruins in 1918, and its two fine gothic churches practically destroyed.   At Montdidier, in 1737, was born the agriculturist Antoine Parmentier, who introduced the potato into France.   It is curious to think of the French kitchen lacking this vital comestible until the second half of the eighteenth century.

The department of the Pas de Calais, due north of the Somme, roughly corresponds in configuration to the old province of Artois, and is a region ill-favoured in scenic interest.   The name of Artois is most generally connected with artesian wells, of which the first was sunk at Lillers in the twelfth century, and with the unyielding Comte d'Artois who ascended the throne of France as Charles X in 1825.   The region is also well-known for its beer and truffles and the delicious trout inhabiting the rivers of the Canche and the Scarpe, which bisect the flat surface of the Pas de Calais.

Arras, the capital, together with Bethune and many other towns in the department, was so shattered during the war as to have lost all artistic interest, although credit and respect must be given to those who undertook the disheartening task of rebuilding them, often in imitation of the originals.   The Hôtel de Ville at Arras is the most notable and thorough attempt in this direction.   The most important towns in the

Pas de Calais fortunate enough to escape irreparable damage were Montreuil-sur-Mer, St. Omer, Boulogne, and Calais. The first of these, lying south of the Boulonnais, is a pretty old fortified town situated on the northern slope of a plateau above the river Canche. The sea originally washed the foot of the plateau below the ramparts, which, to-day, have been converted into the most delightful promenade. Readers of Sterne will recollect that in *A Sentimental Journey* a halt was made at Montreuil-sur-Mer.

The country east of Montreuil towards St. Pol, an ancient market town, is rich and undulating, but northwards, as St. Omer is approached, it is sadly defaced, straggling industrial villages being separated from each other by short stretches of arable land. St. Omer is said to possess the finest church in Artois, but except for the interesting south portal of the fourteenth century, Notre Dame is not of outstanding merit. The interior is overcrowded with *ex votos* and tombs. In the rue St. Bertin is the present military hospital with a venerable English connection. Here, in 1592, the Jesuits opened a school for English Catholics which, after the dissolution of the Society of Jesus, was successively removed to Bruges and Liège, to settle finally at Stonyhurst in Lancashire in 1794. Both Titus Oates and Daniel O'Connell were pupils of this distinguished academy.

Boulogne, the chief fishing-port in France, consists of a lower town on the right bank of the Liane, well known to the English tourist, and of a far more interesting and less frequented Haute Ville which, enclosed by ancient ramparts, stands on a height on the eastern side of the town. Unfortunately many of the buildings within the walls, including the cathedral, date from the last century. The old twelfth-century church of Notre Dame was burnt during the Revolution, largely because it was the shrine of one of the most venerated Madonnas in Europe. This black wooden figure of the Virgin was traditionally supposed to have arrived at Boulogne during the seventh century, seated in an open boat and unattended by any crew.

A connection between England and Boulogne has existed since the reign of Henry VIII, who captured the town in 1544, although he prudently sold it to Charles IX six years later. From 1801 to 1805 Boulogne became the centre of Napoleon's alarming preparations for the invasion of Great Britain, and later in the century it earned an invidious reputation, as far as the English were concerned, as a refuge for debtors and a meeting-place for irascible gentlemen who wished to fight duels.

Calais, which by force of geographical circumstances is the best-known town amongst Britons in France, suffers in reputation from the discomforts of the cross-Channel journey and from the fact that few of its visitors have time to explore its hidden charms. Close to the quays, however, at which the steamers arrive from Dover, lies the really entrancing quarter of Le Courgain in the old town. In its ancient and irregular streets can be enjoyed the sounds of an incomprehensible dialect and the picturesque sight of the fisher-folk in their local costume, which many would only expect to find in the more remote and isolated regions of France.

In the centre of the old town, which is entirely surrounded by water, lies the delightful Place d'Armes in the South Flemish style, reminiscent of Spanish sixteenth-century architecture. The old Hôtel de Ville is a dignified example of the early Louis XV manner, while nearby the gothic church of Notre Dame will surprise the English visitor by its likeness to churches in Kent, particularly in the tower and vaulting. Modern Calais on the west is well laid out and is still noted for its manufacture of tulle and lace.

Calais, which was taken by Edward III in 1347, when the six burghers with halters round their necks offered their lives in order to prevent the destruction of the town, was obstinately held by the English until 1558, when the Duc de Guise expelled the foreign garrison; an event which, in the opinion of Queen Mary Tudor, had an unusual effect upon her heart. From Calais in 1561 Mary Stuart, the widow of François II, embarked for Scotland; here in 1814 Louis XVIII landed to assume the French crown, and in Calais the following year Emma, Lady Hamilton, ended her resourceful life. Near the old Hôtel de Ville once stood the Hôtel Dessein which figures in the opening scene of Sterne's *A Sentimental Journey*.

The most northerly department in France is suitably called the Nord, and its long and amorphous configuration is practically identical with that of French Flanders, which stretched from the North Sea to the foot-hills of the Ardennes. It is a low-lying and flat district, and wide expanses of uninteresting agricultural land divide the great industrial areas of Lille, Douai, and Valenciennes. Like Belgium and Dutch Flanders, the Nord originally belonged to the Countship of Flanders, which, after being united to Burgundy in 1385, passed first under Austrian and then under Spanish rule. The architectural influence of the latter can be studied in this region, particularly at Lille. Finally, in 1713, France secured her share of Flanders, despite the resistance of the Duke of Marlborough and the sullen hostility of its largely alien inhabitants.

Cambrai, which is the most important place in the south of the Nord, was the headquarters of the Crown Prince Ruprecht during the

war, and when the Germans evacuated it in 1918 they heavily mined the
centre of the town.　The resulting explosions and fires left no important monument unscathed.　Nevertheless, the imposing eighteenth-
century cathedral retains a comparatively unimpaired façade, as also,
unluckily, does the hideous Hôtel de Ville, built in the early years of
the Third Republic.　In history Cambrai is famous for the "Paix des
Dames," signed there in 1529 by Louise of Savoy, the mother of
François I, and Margaret of Austria, the aunt of the Emperor Charles V.
Cambrai has been renowned for its linens since the thirteenth century,
when Baptiste de Cambrai invented the fine fabric called "cambric"
by the English and *baptiste* by the French.

North-east of Cambrai lies Valenciennes, on the Scheldt.　Originally
a Roman town named after one of the three Valentinian Emperors, its
name is also connected with its exquisite lace and the homely "valance."
The manufacture of lace began here at the close of the sixteenth and
expired at the beginning of the nineteenth century.　Since then, the
introduction of iron and steel factories has sadly defaced the old town,
of which Watteau and Pater were natives and where Carpeaux modelled
the gilded beauties of the Second Empire.

The country between Valenciennes and Douai is nearly all industrialised, but the latter town, on the canalised Scarpe, is not without
charm and historical interest.　In the sacristy of the principal church
of Notre Dame can be seen a masterpiece of early Renaissance painting
in the beautiful polyptych of Jean Bellegambe, consisting of nine outer
panels representing Christ enthroned and five inner ones depicting the
Trinity surrounded by the Church Triumphant.　The Hôtel de Ville,
although of little architectural importance, has a fifteenth-century
Flemish belfry with chimes which play the cheerful *Air du Gayant* in
honour of the legendary giant whose wicker effigy is paraded through
the streets on July 6th, the *Fête du Gayant.*

Douai was the chief centre of English Catholicism during the reigns
of Queen Elizabeth and James I, and here Cardinal Allen founded his
seminary for young men who were willing to return as priests and risk
the fierce penal laws in their own country.　The "Douai Version,"
or Roman Catholic translation of the Bible into English, was completed
here at that period, the New Testament being published at Rheims in
1582 and the Old Testament at Douai in 1610.

Douai and Valenciennes make the base of an irregular isosceles
triangle, of which the apex is formed by Lille, the old capital of French
Flanders, and now the chief town in the department of the Nord.
Lille, which is the fifth largest town in France, is the centre of one of
the most extensive industrial areas in the country.　Its chief manu-

factures are flax and cotton spinning ("lisle thread"), wool-combing, tobacco, beer, and chemicals.   Its monuments are mainly grouped in the northern quarter of the town, and these can be approached by the delightful Porte du Tournai, an imposing brick erection of the Louis XVI period.   In the Grande Place lies the old Bourse built by Julien Destré in the seventeenth century.   In its exuberant but unrelated ornamentation it is very reminiscent of late Renaissance architecture of Spain.   The Palais des Beaux Arts is one of the finest provincial museums in France, although usually it is unprovided with a catalogue. Apart from an admirable picture-gallery, which ranges in period from Dirk Bouts to Carolus Duran, a native of Lille, its most important possession is the wax-tinted head of a girl, which some critics ascribe to the Roman period and others to the school of Leonardo da Vinci. North-west of the town lies the superb pentagonal citadel which is one of the most impressive and complete of Vauban's fortresses.

During the war Lille enjoyed an invidious reputation amongst German soldiers in the firing line similar to that possessed by Limoges amongst the French rank and file.   The elegant Prussian officers who paraded their fine persons in the town were known as the "heroes of the Lille front," and they were as much despised as the prudent French Staff officers who were said to spend the greater part of their active service at Limoges.

8

CHAPTER IV

THE CHÂTEAU COUNTRY

THE ancient province of Touraine, which is the heart of the château country, corresponds roughly to the modern department of Indre-et-Loire, but for the purposes of this chapter the two adjacent departments, Maine-et-Loire on the west and Loir-et-Cher on the east, are included. The three departments form a group which are strung together by the Loire, which flows through the centre of each.

As with so much of France, the province was for a time linked with England under the Plantagenet King Henry II, but in 1204 Philip Augustus succeeded in uniting it to the French crown. When, during the fifteenth century, the English expelled Charles VII from Paris, he spent the greater part of his time in Tours and in the castles of the surrounding district; from that period dated his love of Touraine, which was shared by the majority of his successors on the throne during the two following centuries.

The frequent presence of the king in the province compelled the noblemen of the court to follow the royal example and reside in the same neighbourhood. For this reason are found the extraordinary number of châteaux which cluster round the banks of the Loire and its tributaries as it passes through Touraine. The builders of these majestic castles were animated by the same spirit which was found in the eighteenth-century landowner in England, a competitive desire to have a larger and more magnificent house than his neighbour. The majority of the châteaux began their histories as mediæval fortresses, but with the coming of the Renaissance they were developed into the ornate buildings which are to be seen to-day. Although so large a number still stand, they are no more than a part of those originally built, and about the countryside bordering the Loire there are ruins, some of considerable size, which are all that remain of important mediæval buildings. In any other district of France these mouldering towers and walls would be considered worthy of careful preservation, while guidebooks would devote paragraphs of notes to their description, but here architecture is cheap, and a mere ruin, unless of exceptional historic or architectural importance, is neglected in favour of the many buildings which are still standing.

57   Château de Courances: the Garden Front

58 The Loire at Saumur

59 Château
d'Amboise from
the Loire

French courtiers traditionally preferred life in Paris or its neighbourhood to the charms of a bucolic existence, but this sentiment was probably less developed in the fifteenth century, and the nobles can have found little hardship in being compelled to live in the lovely country of Touraine. The great valley through which the Loire flows may seem to many as beautiful as any countryside in France, and more romance has in the course of centuries been gathered on its banks than round any river in the world. During the dry months of summer the waters are divided into many little streams, which flow, green and pellucid, amongst the yellow sandbanks and narrow islands covered with tangles of the olive-green willows which thrive in this watery soil. Here and there, where the stream is wide and gently flowing, coloured tents are set up during the summer on the golden strands of sand and shingle, and for a few months some normally deserted stretch of river becomes as animated as a little seaside town. The swift currents, however, are apt to be treacherous, so that bathing in the Loire becomes a pastime which Mr. Baedeker, had he ever envisaged his readers doing anything so unseemly and so rash, would certainly not have advised for ladies.

In winter there may be a very different picture. The gentle streams join into one strong torrent which fills the wide bed from side to side; often the waters rise so high that they flow over the islands, bending and tearing the willows, and the high dykes, which border the river for the greater part of its journey through Touraine, are tested to the utmost to keep the flood from the wide expanse of low-lying country, which in places extends for miles on either side. The soil in this part of Touraine is not rich, but trees grow well, and since in France no space is wasted, the valley of the Loire and of the streams which flow into it is well clothed with timber. There is none of the English neglect about this well-wooded country : trees are accepted as a crop equally with corn, and are planted and tended to produce the maximum return. Although a certain natural picturesqueness may thereby be lacking, the well-grown trees are a continual pleasure to the eye. This is not a first-class agricultural district, but it is saved from possible poverty by the grapes which are grown in small vineyards on the gentle slopes bordering the valley. Few of the more important wines come from this neighbourhood, but in Touraine and to a greater degree in the adjacent province of Anjou are produced those delicious light wines which, so tantalisingly, are seldom transported to England.

The peaceful landscape of the province melts naturally into the dignified and quiet charm of Tours, the capital. There is an air of safety and domestic security about the town which, apart from the purity of the local accent, makes it a particularly suitable place for the young English student to learn the language. The *Urbs Turonum* of the Romans was built on the south bank of the river at a point where the stream is broken by several considerable islands, and owing to the distance from the opposite shore has developed entirely on this side of the river. The haphazard mediæval plan of narrow streets which grew up along the river bank was arbitrarily bisected during the latter half of the eighteenth century by a fine straight road, which passes without deviation through the town and over the handsome stone bridge across the Loire. Round the southern extremity of this rue Nationale grew the new quarter, which has been laid out on good spacious lines, while the old town was thus divided into two distinct parts. On the west side are many streets of picturesque houses dating from the sixteenth and seventeenth centuries; amongst them stands the modern basilica dedicated to St. Martin, a saint famous both in England and France, who towards the end of the fourth century became the third bishop of Tours. His tomb is in the crypt below the choir of the basilica. On the east side are the two major ornaments of the town, the cathedral and the former archbishop's palace, a charming eighteenth-century building which now houses a museum and picture-gallery. The cathedral is one of the finest in France despite a mixture of styles which extends from the thirteenth to the sixteenth century, during which period architecture passed through the full gamut of gothic development. The façade, which was the latest part to be built, is a magnificent and exuberant example of the early Renaissance style, when gothic tradition still dominated the classical innovations. Round the cathedral are streets and shady squares of handsome houses built in a simple eighteenth-century style.

On the eastern outskirts of Tours stands the castle of Plessis-les-Tours, a building in stone and brick dating from late in the fifteenth century. Architecturally its claims are perhaps rather modest, but it is historically interesting, since it was built by Louis XI and became his favourite residence. The king died here on August 30th, 1483.

East of Tours, the river valley is narrowed to the width of a mile or so by a long line of limestone hills, which rise in steep white cliffs from close to the southern bank. In dominant positions on the edge of the cliffs stand two famous châteaux, Amboise and Chaumont, the former rising above the roofs of a little town which clusters round its lower ramparts, the latter standing alone amongst the hanging woods clothing the steep slopes below it. Roads pass along either bank of the river, and from the north road there is a fine view across the water to the wooded ridges, punctuated with these splendid groups of towers and bastions.

Before reaching the neighbourhood of Amboise, the north road passes through the village of Vouvray, a name which gives a thrill to the lovers of the excellent wines of Touraine. The grapes are grown all about the slopes of the adjacent hills in small vineyards, the majority of which are no more than a few acres in extent, and the wine is brought to maturity in the caves and tunnels with which these calcareous hills are riddled. All along the road are the wine-dealers' yards and presses, while close behind rise the low cliffs in which nature has so obligingly provided free and temperate cellarage. These caves are also sometimes used as dwelling-houses, in the same way that they are in the valley of the Seine; a wall, with a door and perhaps a window, is built across the opening, and a chimney is tunnelled through the rock to emerge surprisingly at the top of the cliff. It is said that these troglodytic cottages are both dry and warm, but it is difficult to believe that they could satisfy any but the most unexacting standards.

A long bridge connects the north road with the south at Amboise, coming into the little town directly below the walls of the castle. This great building, which forms such a magnificent group with its splendid façade rising from fifteenth-century towers and bastions, is of particular architectural interest, since it represents some of the earliest Renaissance architecture in France. It is a manner which is not naturally congenial to the English, since we have no close counterpart in our own country through which we could grow accustomed to so exuberant and ornate a style. But it has undoubtedly a rare beauty of line and detail combined with freedom and invention such as is not to be found at any other period.

The Renaissance was brought to France by Charles VIII, who returned from several military years in Italy in 1493 and founded the "School of Amboise." He had begun the rebuilding of the castle, which was to serve as a model for the greater number of the châteaux in the district, two years earlier, and work was continued by his successor, Louis XII, after his death through an accident at Amboise in 1498. This unfortunate event took place in the enclosed garden within the walls of the castle; Charles was passing through a low doorway, which still stands, when he struck his head against the stone lintel with such force that he cracked his skull and died. It was an humiliating death for a monarch.

The most terrible event in the history of Amboise came in the middle of the following century, when hundreds of Huguenots who had conspired against the king were hung from the iron balconies on the façade overlooking the river. It is a story which appeals strongly to the castle guides, and visitors may rest assured that they will be spared no detail of the harrowing and bloodcurdling story of the massacre.

A few miles east, on the same ridge, stands Chaumont, a redoubtable fortress defended by vast circular towers at the corners and entrance, which was begun in 1473. Although started as a purely defensive gothic building, one can detect the coming of the Renaissance a quarter of a century later in details of doorways and window surrounds. The rooms within these formidable walls have decoration and furniture dating from the sixteenth century, at which time the castle was more or less compulsorily transferred to Diane de Poitiers by Catherine de Medici in exchange for the more attractive Château de Chenonceaux. Amongst the superb furnishings are the beds of these two bitterly opposed women: there could be no more suitable mementoes of their rivalry.

Chenonceaux, from which Diane was successfully ousted after the death of her protector Henri II in 1535, lies a few miles south of Chaumont in a romantic position astride the river Cher. The original house consisted of a squat, early sixteenth-century rectangular block built on arches which rise from the waters of the river; to this nucleus was added a bridge connecting the château with the south bank, so that Diane might indulge her passion for the chase over the low-lying country beyond the river. When Catherine de Medici secured the house, she built, from the designs of De l'Orme, a long gallery on Diane's bridge, thus making the transit even more easy, and also perhaps providing an inspiration for Inigo Jones when, about eighty years later, he was called upon to design a house for Henrietta Maria at Greenwich which would enable the queen to pass from park to waterfront without crossing the Dover road. The solution in both cases is the same.

In the rising open country south of the Cher lies the magnificent château of Valençay, which will always be connected with the name of France's most outstanding statesman, Talleyrand, and is still owned by his collateral descendants. It is said to be the largest inhabited house in France. After indulging in an orgy of early Renaissance architecture, it is with some relief that one views the restrained classical proportions of the long seventeenth-century façade which looks on to the park. Here also, however, the basis was sixteenth-century, and the Louis XIV building is framed by domed towers of the earlier period. The park adjacent to the house is now given up to a private zoo, and wallabies, ostriches, and kangaroos prance on the greensward where the enigmatic M. de Talleyrand was wont to take his dignified walks.

North of Valençay a wide expanse of low-lying country, watered by the Cher and its two tributaries the Nahon and the Sauldre, stretches away to the little town of Romorantin, which is built about the two branches of the latter river. The town contains a much restored

60   Blois: the Courtyard of the Château

61   Château de Chenonceaux, bridging the Cher

62   The Greatest of the Châteaux: Chambord

63   Chambord: a Detail of the Roof-line

castle and, more interesting, several sixteenth-century timber-framed houses; one is ornamented with a trellis pattern of beams with a filling of brick, and others are decorated with elaborate gothic carving.

The district surrounding Romorantin and stretching eastward into the neighbouring province of Berry is known as La Sologne, an area which, until the latter half of the nineteenth century, was a deserted marshy waste. Arthur Young, with the knowledge of the expert agriculturist, wrote in 1788: "Sologne is one of the poorest and most unimproved provinces of the Kingdom. The soil is retentive of water to such a degree that every ditch and hole was full of it." Drainage, the planting of pine-trees, and the application of scientific methods have, however, produced a remarkable change in the countryside, and Mr. Young would undoubtedly be greatly impressed by the evidence of agricultural prosperity which is to be seen to-day.

Within a few miles of each other, near the northern boundaries of the Sologne, lie two famous châteaux, Chambord and Cheverny; they built one a hundred years later than the other, and so form a useful example of the progress of architectural taste during the sixteenth century. The former was begun in 1523 by François 1er in a marshy clearing in the Forest of Boulogne, and is the largest château in the Loire country. The great walls and towers, which are designed on a strictly symmetrical plan, rise with little ornamentation to a roof-line of the wildest elaboration: gables, dormers, chimneys, cupolas, pinnacles cluster above the rectangular central block in a riot of ordered confusion. To walk over the flat of the roof amongst these remarkable erections is like wandering in a cave of giant stalagmites.

The interior is curiously arranged, with a great open hall in the shape of a cross on each floor and the living-rooms disposed in the angles. In the centre, two stone stairways, entwined but never meeting, spiral from ground to roof. Of domestic comfort there can never have been a trace, and one can picture poor Stanislas of Poland shivering in these stone-vaulted halls during his sojourn here in the middle of the eighteenth century, and later the embarrassment of Maréchal Berthier on being presented with this gigantic white elephant by his grateful Emperor.

Cheverny, which is surrounded by a pretty park, is far more attractive: it is less ostentatious, it has magnificent interior decoration, and above all, since it is still inhabited, it has not lost its soul. It was begun in 1634, and shows throughout the uncertainties of the Renaissance disappearing before the full understanding of classic principles. The exterior is not a great success, but the beautiful rooms with their appropriate furnishings are a revelation of seventeenth-century splendour.

On the steeply rising ground which slopes from the north bank of the Loire is Blois, its brick and stone houses mounting to the great castle which dominates this little town in the same manner that for centuries it dominated the early history of France. A building which dates from such various periods can hardly form a successful or harmonious whole, and each wing is best viewed without the context of its neighbours. There is the low Louis XII wing in brick and stone through which one passes into the central courtyard; to the left on entering is a rather nondescript fifteenth-century gallery; on the right the tremendous building which François Ier created round the existing mediæval fortress; and opposite the splendid classical façade designed by Mansard for Gaston d'Orléans in 1635. It is interesting to note how far more successfully Mansard had assimilated the true classical principles than had Boyer, the architect of contemporary Cheverny.

The interior of the Gaston wing was never completed, and now houses in its empty shell a large public library, but the remainder of the castle has been restored with the usual alarming French thoroughness, and walls, ceilings, and pillars now blaze with nineteenth-century replicas of fifteenth-century stencilling. The event which, above all others, is connected with Blois is the murder of the Duc de Guise in the presence of Henri III in 1588. As with sensational events in other châteaux, it is a story well told by the guides.

The castle is not the only object of interest in this congested hillside town; the cathedral is a fine example of *flamboyant* gothic, while adjacent to it is the former bishop's palace, a charming classical building designed by Gabriel and now housing a museum. From the terraces of the garden there is a magnificent view over the roofs of the town to the gleaming waters of the Loire and the wooded country beyond.

At Blois, as in most other towns of consequence in France, the bishop's palace and the surrounding gardens, which were abandoned by the church during the last century owing to reduced revenues, have proved of inestimable value to the inhabitants. The buildings, which in the majority of cases date from the eighteenth century, form excellent museums and picture-galleries, often far outshining in merit their rather haphazard contents, while the surroundings, which have probably been cultivated and tended for centuries, became, without alteration, splendid public gardens.

North of Blois stretches the Plateau de la Beauce, a deserted area of country rather bleak and treeless except for the Forest of Blois near the town and the Forest of Marchenoir on the east. The northern boundary is formed by the river Le Loir, which is so gratuitously confusing with its parallel neighbour La Loire, which it eventually joins south of Angers. On this river is the town of Vendôme, which has given its beautiful name to many royal dukes of France since the title was granted by Henri IV to his son by Gabrielle d'Estrées. The castle, which stands above the town, is now ruined, though the keep and part of the fortifications still stand to show its considerable extent; but the principal ornament is the church dedicated to the Trinity. The west façade is one of the finest examples of *flamboyant* gothic in the country: tracery and ornamentation of a lacelike lightness rise to a bewildering riot of pinnacles, crockets, turrets, and flying buttresses. The result is a triumph of doubtful architectural taste. Close to the church stands an isolated belfry dating from the twelfth century, which by its simple and dignified lines emphasises the frivolity of its neighbour.

The river Loir flows westward through a valley of calcareous hills which have their usual accompaniment of caves and grottoes, many of which form economical habitations for the hardy peasants, as in other parts of the country.

With the exception of the river valleys, the country on the east side of Tours reaches a modest altitude of a few hundred feet, but on the west the Loire valley opens out into a great low-lying plain which stretches away beyond Angers and Nantes to the coast of the Bay of Biscay. The volume of the river as it passes through Touraine is considerably increased by the waters of the Cher, the Indre, and the Vienne, all of which finish their long courses from the great central plateau within a few miles of each other. The country south of the Loire is channelled by a network of waterways which join, separate, and rejoin, forming intricate groups of islands and peninsulas which connect Tours to Angers like a tangled cluster of cords. In this area are to be found an even greater number of famous châteaux than there are on the higher reaches of the Loire; so close together do they lie, indeed, that the visitor becomes dazed and probably surfeited by this glut of fine architecture. There is barely a decent pause as he drives from one to another, and it is possible, if fatigue allows, to visit nearly a dozen in a day.

A careful description of each would be unbearably tedious, so a passing reference to only a few must suffice. Close to Tours is the grim fortress of Luynes, the thirteenth and fifteenth-century towers of which rise from a steep hill above the village, which clusters close to the northern bank of the river. It is still inhabited by the dukes of that name. Passing the ruins of the Castle of Cinq-Mars, with its curious square tower, the road comes to Langeais, a formidable fifteenth-century château standing in the centre of a little town; during the latter half of the last century the castle was fully restored and

9

furnished with appropriate period furniture by a public-spirited M. Jacques Siegfried, who bequeathed it to the Institût des Beaux Arts, by whom it is maintained as a museum.   It is, indeed, quite unsuited to any other purpose.

South of the Loire and within a few miles of Tours is Villandry, which, with its superb garden, will seem to many by far the most attractive of this group of châteaux.   The house is a particularly sympathetic example of the François 1er style, and the formal garden, which has been remade on the original lines, is one of the finest of its sort in the world, probably being only surpassed by the great garden at Herrenhausen near Hanover.   It shows a lay-out of the early seventeenth century before the revolutionary ideas of Le Nôtre altered the whole intention of garden design, when, however large the extent, the effect was intimate and the range of the eye was restricted to a rectangle enclosed by a clipped hedge.   The topiary work at Villandry is superb, with one square given up to gothic and another to classical designs, but the most fascinating part of the lay-out is the great area of kitchen garden, which is subdivided by paths into numerous enclosures surrounded by dwarf box hedges;   within these formal frames the vegetables are grown, making as pretty a piece of coloured pattern as any parterre of flowers.

A few miles further west, in a close group, lie three important châteaux: Azay-le-Rideau, an early Renaissance building surrounded on three sides by the waters of the Indre; Ussé, also sixteenth-century, with an enchanting wing added towards the end of the seventeenth century by Vauban, which shows that the celebrated designer of fortresses was a loss to the field of domestic architecture; and, thirdly, Chinon, a vast ruin of which some walls and towers still stand covering the level top of a wide hill above the Vienne.   It was at Chinon that Joan of Arc had her first meeting with the French king, Charles VII, on March 6th, 1429, and the well-known scene took place when the king, partly in mockery, partly to test her powers, endeavoured to confuse her regarding his identity.

South of Chinon, in a bleak countryside of flat arable fields with barely a hedge or grove of trees to break the wide landscape, is the interesting but seldom visited little town of Richelieu, which was built by the famous cardinal in the early seventeenth century.   It consists of a rectangle entirely surrounded by a moat and high walls.   From handsome gateways, semi-fortified, semi-classical, straight streets pass through the town, dividing it into symmetrical divisions; where they cross are two considerable squares lined with the classical stone façades of modest two-storeyed houses.   Although the appearance of the houses in the squares and streets is now rather marred by shop signs and advertisements, there seems to have been remarkably little structural alteration to the original design, so that it would not be difficult to re-establish it as a unique and miniature example of a seventeenth-century town.

On the south side, a gateway of particular grandeur leads to the site of the château. The park remains, but the formal avenues, glades, and canals lead to no more than the moat and the great moulded stones of the foundations; roses now bloom where the cardinal's magnificent palace originally stood. The estate has for some years been the property of the Sorbonne.

Richelieu lies close to the southern borders of Touraine, and a few miles to the west the province gives way to Anjou—or, to apply the modern names, the department of Indre-et-Loire gives way to Maine-et-Loire. Just within the boundaries of Anjou and close to the junction of the Vienne with the Loire is the Abbey of Fontevrault, which contains in its church the tombs of two kings and two queens of England. The abbey buildings are now rather inconveniently converted into a house of "detention and correction," but visitors are able to inspect the church and the cloisters without a glimpse of the unfortunate inmates. The abbey is rather over-restored, but nevertheless is a singularly perfect and beautiful example of Romanesque building; the tall, closely set arcade of pillars which surround the apse of the chancel give an almost theatrical effect of light and beauty when seen from the comparative darkness of the nave. In the transept are the twelfth-century tombs, surmounted by recumbent gothic figures, of Henry II and his wife, Eleanor of Guyenne, of Richard Cœur-de-Lion, who died in 1199 when beseiging the castle of Chalus, and of Isabella of Angoulême, wife of the unlucky King John.

When the church and tombs, which had fallen into a sad state of disrepair, were restored in the last century, Napoleon III tactfully wrote to Queen Victoria to enquire whether she would have any objection to "the English St. Denis" returning to Catholic worship. The Queen raised no difficulties, "not wishing that affront should be offered in her name to the pious and patriotic wishes of the Kings, her illustrious predecessors of the House of Anjou." It was a considerable concession on the part of Her Majesty.

The cloisters which adjoin the church date from the sixteenth century and are of interest, since one walk is gothic while the remainder show strong Renaissance tendencies. The twelfth-century kitchen of the abbey still stands, a curious circular, conical building in which the cooking was done over fires in recesses round the walls, while the smoke emerged from cupolas above them and in the peak of the roof.

9*

The only large town on the long sweep of waterways between Tours and Angers is Saumur, which stands on the southern bank of the Loire. Seen from across the river it presents a most attractive picture, with its long line of houses partially concealed behind a row of neatly pleached trees, while on the eastern side great bastions rise from wooded slopes to support the high terrace on which stands the castle. The latter is so placed that it commands the confluence of the Thouet and the Loire, and from the terrace there is a magnificent view up and down a wide stretch of river and across the water to the low-lying plains of Maine-et-Loire beyond.

The castle as it now stands is the product of intensive restoration, but the spirit of the original fifteenth-century building has been well maintained, and the tall octagonal corner-towers and high façades crowned with dormer-windows in the steep-pitched roofs make an effective group. The interior is architecturally unimportant and contains an extensive museum of rather varying merit. On the third floor eight galleries have been formed which are given up to a museum of everything to do with the horse and the equestrian arts. The several skeletons of famous horses which the rooms contain have a certain melancholy interest.

Saumur is undoubtedly the most suitable place for a museum of this nature, since in the lower part of the town is the famous cavalry school. The young gentlemen of the academy are housed in handsome barracks of simple classical design dating from the middle of the eighteenth century; between the barracks and the river is a vast tree-bordered parade ground which has been the scene of many horse shows and kindred beanos since the first exhibition was given before the Duchesse de Berry in 1828.

The department of Maine-et-Loire, on the eastern edge of which Saumur lies, corresponds roughly to the ancient province of Anjou, the heritage of the Plantagenet Kings of England. It is a more fertile country than Touraine, and the gently rolling hills, divided into small arable fields, produce heavy crops of corn. Artichokes, their silver leaves making an unexpectedly beautiful colour-scheme against the deep red earth, are one of the principal products of the district, but wine is the most famous. Vineyards are small; thus the wine which is the output of individual enterprise is apt to vary greatly from year to year. This uncertainty may be one of the reasons why the excellent wines of Anjou are so seldom seen in England rather than that they will not travel, since they make without harm, it is said, the long journey to the French possessions in Cochin China.

The capital of Anjou is the large town of Angers, which lies away

64, 65　Garden Architecture at Villandry

66   Château de Falaise

67   Old Houses at Tours

from the banks of the Loire on the Maine, close to the confluence of the Loir and the Mayenne. It is now an important industrial centre, and must have more than doubled in size during the last half-century. The French, however, have a peculiar gift for enlarging mediæval towns with commercial suburbs without destroying or, indeed, even altering the original atmosphere. Where in England any country town, such for example as Northampton or Leicester, is immediately ruined architecturally by the advent of commercial prosperity, in France the old towns slumber on apparently oblivious of the remarkable developments on their outskirts.

This is essentially the case at Angers. The main square, the Place du Ralliement, contains larger cafés and shows rather more animation than it would if it were the centre of no more than a market-town, but the network of narrow streets leading from it to the cathedral and the castle fully retain their ancient air. The cathedral, which is a splendid example of twelfth and thirteenth-century gothic, stands finely on high ground overlooking the town. The interior is very splendid and is much enhanced by remarkable twelfth-century stained glass in the top windows and fifteenth-century glass in the transepts. Adjoining is the former bishop's palace, which now contains the unparalleled collection of tapestries for which Angers is famous. The earliest is a set of twenty dating from 1377 representing the Apocalypse, and there are also examples from many other periods up to the eighteenth century.

In the old streets of this part of the town are to be found some interesting early houses: there are the Logie Pincé, with a handsome stone façade in the Renaissance style and several fifteenth and sixteenth-century timber-framed buildings of unusual height and construction. Some of the latter are decorated with elaborate carving of figures, flowers, and leaves; any visitor contemplating their interesting façades will almost inevitably have indicated to him by a passing Angevin some particularly lively scenes which are to be discovered amongst the riot of ornamentation.

The castle stands close to the banks of the Maine, and is a tremendous example of a thirteenth-century fortress. From a deep dry moat the curtain-walls, punctuated at regular intervals by seventeen robust towers, rise to a great height and present an aspect of complete invincibility. This building shows clearly how far more advanced at that period were the arts of defence than those of attack: it is most unfortunate that during the passing centuries the balance should have been reversed. The interior of the castle is now used as a barracks and contains little of interest.

The province of Anjou is less rich in châteaux than Touraine, but it contains a considerable number within some miles' radius of Angers which are worth visiting, though in many cases only the exteriors can be seen.   There is Serrant, a Renaissance building belonging to the family of La Trémouille, and the châteaux of Plessis-Macé and Plessis-Bourré, while further north is Bazouges-sur-Loir, with its massive machicolated gatehouse.   But the most interesting of all is the Château de Brissac, which lies south of Angers, beyond the valley of the Loire, in a pretty, fertile country of arable fields and vineyards.   As with so many French houses, the immediate surroundings are painfully inadequate, and the vast building of mediæval towers and high Renaissance façades rises from a little garden and meadow which would be more suited to a modest villa.

The interior is extremely interesting and contains a great number of rooms which have remained materially unchanged since the early seventeenth century.   Walls four yards thick support high ceilings the heavy beams of which are elaborately painted in colours, huge stone canopied fireplaces break the expanse of tapestry with which the rooms are lined, and massive furniture dating from the reign of Louis XIII stands on the wide oak boards of the floors.   It is very impressive, but exceedingly uncomfortable.

CHAPTER V

THE ÎLE-DE-FRANCE AND THE CATHEDRAL COUNTRY

THE ancient province of the Île-de-France had an amorphous shape and a curious name. It stretched from Étampes in the south to the Belgian frontier, while Mantes and Provins were its most western and eastern towns of any importance. The configuration of the region was determined by political or perhaps feudal considerations, since it included principally the country round Paris which was finally subdued by the early kings of the House of Capet during the tenth and eleventh centuries. In fact, the name of "France" was first used to designate this small territory, which, with Paris as its centre, was destined to extend its rule to the whole of the former Roman province of Gaul. The beautiful names of Bonneuil-en-France, Roissy-en-France, and Châtenay-en-France are romantic relics of that distant age when embryonic France was confined within such narrow boundaries. The term "île" to denote a province is at first misleading, since in the modern interpretation of the word the present departments of the Aisne, the Oise, the Seine-et-Oise and Seine-et-Marne, which are identical in area to the Île-de-France, can in no sense be said to be situated on an island. In the early Middle Ages, however, *île* was a French word applied not only to islands and peninsulas (*presqu'îles*) but also to stretches of land wholly or partially surrounded by rivers. This designation was particularly appropriate to this territory round Paris, since its boundaries were broadly defined by the rivers of the Seine, the Oise, the Aisne, the Ourcq, and the Marne. The name of the province was therefore pertinent both geographically and historically, since not only was the Île-de-France isolated by five great rivers from the contiguous country, but also it emphasised the vital fact that the Île was the root from which grew modern France.

The first known mention of the Île-de-France, under that name, was made by Froissart in the fifteenth century, and it was during the last quarter of that century that the confines of the province became fixed. Three hundred years earlier, however, the Île had emerged as the centre of the growing French kingdom when Philippe-Auguste added Normandy, Anjou, Maine, and Touraine to his dominions; but during the Hundred Years War the Île suffered from frequent invasions by the

English, and it was the storm centre of the "Jacquerie" in the middle of the fourteenth century. This widespread rebellion of the peasants against the tyranny of the nobles and the privations they were enduring in the course of the war was responsible for great excesses committed on both persons and property. During the successful but short period of the revolt the country was ravaged by the "Jacques," who indulged in torture and incendiarism. Froissart records how a woman of gentle birth was compelled to watch her husband being roasted on a spit, her children then being compelled to eat their father's flesh. This disorderly behaviour on the part of the lower classes united for a time the military leaders of England and France, and in the subsequent suppression of the "Jacquerie" it was estimated that twenty thousand peasants were put to the sword.

The rebellion was finally extinguished in 1358, and the English and French, greatly scandalised by this vulgar interruption, settled down to the more agreeable pastime of a feudal war. The result was, however, highly unpropitious for the Île-de-France, since in 1421 Henry V occupied the whole province and in the following year his son was proclaimed King of France in Paris. But the English, under the Regency of the Duke of Bedford, only held the Île for fifteen years, after which they were finally ejected by Joan of Arc, and in 1437 "Charles le Victorieux" was enabled to regain his capital. These long years of war and rebellion inevitably accustomed the inhabitants of the Île-de-France to the proximity of death, and this popularisation of life's only certainty found artistic outlet in the great number and variety of "Danses Macabres" which were painted or carved in so many churches and cemeteries in northern France and elsewhere. The early printing-presses also published them. The preoccupation with death was given continued expression in various forms until the middle of the sixteenth century: of these, one of the most famous is the sculptured effigy of Eustache de Croy in Notre Dame at St. Omer. This bishop, who died in 1538, is portrayed meditating profoundly on a marble replica of his own skeleton.

The Île-de-France only enjoyed a century of peace after the Hundred Years War before being engulfed, with many other parts of the country, in the religious controversy which later led to the Wars of Religion; and in so far as Jean Calvin was born at Noyon in the Île in 1509, that province must bear some responsibility for the ecclesiastical differences of the period. The inhabitants, however, remained on the whole faithful to the Catholic Church and, in company with the citizens of Paris, oppressed with vigour the adherents of reform. In 1567 the Prince de Condé was able to revenge this persecution of his co-religion-

68   Versailles: "Le Roi Soleil"

69   The Palace of St. Germain

70   Malmaison: the Country House of Joséphine

71   Compiègne: the Palace of Marie-Louise

ists by ravaging the country in the neighbourhood of Paris, but his defeat and death at the Battle of St. Denis saved the capital from a similar fate.   The conversion of Henri IV in 1593 was probably as welcome to the inhabitants of the Île-de-France for temporal as for spiritual considerations.

Once again, as after the Hundred Years War, the Île was allowed to enjoy a period of comparative peace despite the constant wars of the Louis XIV period.   But the Revolution naturally inflamed a province so dependent on Paris, and it is interesting to contrast the unwillingness of the people of the Île to embrace the tenets of Calvinism with the eagerness with which they welcomed the extinction of the old régime. With a fickleness, however, which has often distinguished the Gallic temperament, Napoleon was as popular in the Île as anywhere in France, and the tenacity of the inhabitants was proved during the calamitous campaign of 1814.   The Prussians in their advance on Paris committed the anticipated excesses, and the *franc-tireurs* in the Île-de-France responded with characteristic bravery, particularly during the Battle of Montereau, in which the villagers participated from their windows and roofs.   Again in 1870 the province was entirely occupied by the Germans, and more than forty years later, on September 3rd, 1914, a detachment of Uhlans, on the summit of Montmélian, gazed with a reasoned expectation towards the distant silhouette of the Sacré Cœur and the Eiffel Tower.   Montmélian, in the Île, is thirty kilometres from Paris, and it was one of the nearest approaches the Germans made to the capital of France.

The landscape of the Île-de-France cannot be said to be beautiful, although it is superior in scenic interest to its near neighbours, Artois and Picardy, which provinces, as a result of an unkind nature and successive wars, possess a countryside as hideous as any in Europe.   The Île has certainly flat and unstimulating scenery, but it is renowned for its magnificent forests, of which those of Compiègne and Fontainebleau form great barriers of woodland north and south of Paris.   The former forest covers an area of fifty-five square miles, and it is dissected by as many as twelve hundred and fifty miles of avenues and hunting-paths cleared by the Kings of France to facilitate the pleasures of the chase. There is perhaps more arboreal variety in the forest of Fontainebleau, where the oak, the birch, the beech, the hornbeam, the holly, and the juniper form a motley foliage of particular beauty in spring and autumn. Great clumps of ancient trees are often broken by picturesque groups of sandstone rocks and expanses of heath, on which herds of deer can sometimes be seen grazing and where the unwelcome adder is by no means uncommon.   The number of walks to be enjoyed in this forest is legion, and should a visitor be prompted to take one on a Saturday in winter, he may be sufficiently fortunate or unfortunate, according to his point of view, to witness the progress of the historic *chasse au cerf*.

Of the smaller forests Chantilly, which covers an area of over five thousand acres, is mainly composed of oaks, birches, and limes, with some beautiful clumps of conifers. Numerous roads intersect it, mostly covered with sand for the convenience of horses, since Chantilly is the Newmarket of France. The Forest of Marly is similar in acreage and timber to that of Chantilly, and here the President of the French Republic preserves some of the pheasants for his hospitable and exhilarating shoots. Two other lovely forests to which the public has access are those of St. Germain and Sénart. The former, occupying the loop of the Seine between St. Germain and Poissy, is entirely surrounded by walls, and covers nearly a thousand acres. The delightful little forest of Sénart, near Brunoy, of which the Marquisate was given to Wellington by Louis XVIII, is carpeted in May with lilies of the valley.

The quiet charm of the landscape of the Île-de-France, with its long straight roads, distant, flat views, and wide rivers of the Seine, the Marne, the Oise, and the Thérain, which dissect the fertile plains, has been depicted throughout the centuries by some of the greatest artists in France. Jean Fouquet in the fifteenth century painted in his large canvases many exquisite backgrounds in miniature of the environs of Paris. The Renaissance painters were too occupied with Italian art to be interested in their own natural surroundings, but Watteau and his pupils Lancret and Pater painted in their *Fêtes Champêtres*, although from a somewhat idealised aspect, many of the great parks of the Île-de-France.

It was, however, during the early years of the reign of King Louis-Philippe that the Île became not only a favourite subject for artists but also the home of the most famous group of landscape painters of the period. It was in Barbizon, lying in the heart of the Forest of Fontainebleau, that they formed their artistic centre, and called their school of painting after the name of this little town. The founders of the "School of Barbizon" were the forest-lover Théodore Rousseau and the more famous Jean Millet, whose "Angelus" and "The Reapers" suffered in later years a similar fate to that of many a good tune played on a barrel-organ. Corot has been regarded as a member of the School of Barbizon, and, amongst other works, showed his appreciation of the Île-de-France by his well-known and beautiful picture of Mantes. Diaz, who, like Rousseau, painted chiefly in the woodlands, and Daubigny, who specialised in subjects on the borders of the Oise, were also exponents of the school.   Two English names must not be forgotten amongst the prolific artists at Barbizon: that of William Morris Hunt, perhaps a rather minor star, and of Alfred Sisley, born in Paris of English parents, one of the greatest of the Impressionists and to-day considered far superior both in vision and technique to any of the School of Barbizon, with the debatable exception of Corot.   Many of Sisley's finest works were painted on the borders of the Loing, a wide and pleasant river which, rising in the south of the Orléanais, flows gracefully into the Seine by Fontainebleau.

The artists who worked in the Île-de-France cannot be left without mentioning three painters who, with varied inspiration and degrees of artistic ability, rejoiced in the scenic and romantic possibilities of the province without belonging to the School of Barbizon.   Of these Puvis de Chavannes, whose elevation of mind sadly impaired the brilliancy of his palette, placed the emotionless figures in his frescoes in the Sorbonne and in the Panthéon against a faded backcloth of the Île-de-France.   His famous "Bois Sacré," however, depicts in an emasculated manner the magnificent growth and variety of timber in the province.   Far different in this treatment of the Île was Claude Monet, who in his earlier style painted in such translucent colours the banks of the Seine between Mantes and Argenteuil.   Pierre-Auguste Renoir, perhaps the greatest artist of his period both for the catholicity of his subjects and the diversity of his styles, used the Île-de-France as a background for several of his conversational masterpieces.   Of these, the most fascinating and renowned is "Le Déjeuner des Canotiers à Bougival."   Painted in the early 'eighties, this depicts a party of hirsute oarsmen with their eager lady-companions, who, protected by a friendly awning, are grouped round a sumptuous luncheon table laid out by the lush banks of the Seine.

In considering the more important towns and places of interest in the Île-de-France, two liberties will be taken.   The first is that of including, for the sake of convenience, a few towns in the Orléanais, which to-day is covered by the departments of Loiret and Eure-et-Loir, lying immediately to the south of the Île; and the second is that of excluding any description of Paris apart from Notre Dame—an omission for which the reader will no doubt invent a kindly excuse.

The closer and more remote neighbourhood of Paris can be the more easily considered in two circles of arbitrary circumference, of which Sceaux, due south of the capital, will be the first point of interest within the smaller circle.   This pretty little town is celebrated for its pure, bracing air and for the superb view to be obtained from its château across the river Bièvre and the Bois de Verrières.   Of the great seventeenth-century château which Perrault built for Colbert no traces now remain, and its place has been taken by a self-conscious erection in the Louis-Philippe style.   It now houses a delightful collection of pictures and drawings, many depicting the life in the old château, where the Duchesse de Maine held her court early in the eighteenth century and where Voltaire wrote several of his tragedies.   Fortunately, much of the lay-out has been preserved, with some fine canals and avenues.   Near Sceaux lies a pleasure-resort rejoicing in the fanciful name of Robinson.   Here in many restaurants meals for the adventurous can be served high up on platforms amongst the branches of the great chestnut-trees which are such a feature of the neighbourhood.   The quality of the food as well as the method of eating it seem far removed from the simple existence of Robinson Crusoe, after whom Robinson was so gracefully named during the Romantic enthusiasm of the early nineteenth century.

A little west of Sceaux lies Versailles, which is a constellation of too great importance and renown to be mentioned in these pages.   Southwest of Versailles is situated Rambouillet, now the country residence of the President of the French Republic.   The château was originally built in the fourteenth century, but only one machicolated tower remains of this early erection, and frequent restorations have succeeded in destroying any period character the building may have possessed. It is now an amorphous red-brick construction with five flanking towers of stone.   The interior is dignified, as is only fitting for its august occupier, and many of the rooms are furnished with panelling and tapestries of the sixteenth and seventeenth centuries.   The park of the château is laid out in a curious medley of styles.   Parterres and quincunx plantations contrast strangely with a rough garden in the so-called English style and a beautiful avenue of Louisiana cypresses, which are said to be unique in Europe.   The château has witnessed some memorable events in French history.   Here, for example, François 1ʳᵉ died in 1547, and here Charles X signed his abdication in 1830.   It is also said that this most finical of monarchs, despite his unenviable position during the July Revolution, on finding that the table at which he was asked to dine was oval in shape, insisted that it should be made square before he would sit down, since he did not consider that an oval table possessed a distinct enough head for the King of France.

Some distance north of Rambouillet and due west of Paris lies St. Germain-en-Laye, with its royal château now housing the Musée d'Antiquités Nationales.   Frequent restorations, the last being concluded in 1902, have sadly impaired the architectural interest of this building, which was originally erected by Louis the Fat in the twelfth century.   Burnt to the ground during one of the ravaging expeditions of the Black Prince and rebuilt by Charles V and François 1er, the château became a cavalry school under the Empire, a barrack during the Bourbon restoration, a penitentiary under Louis-Philippe, and a museum during the reign of Napoleon III.   There are many English connections with St. Germain, since Queen Henrietta Maria lived there during the Cromwellian period and James II and his queen, Mary of Modena, lived and died there early in the eighteenth century.   The château has also the doubtful distinction of having had the Treaty of St. Germain, between Austria and the Allied Powers, signed within its walls.   It is more pleasant to recollect that in the town of St. Germain-en-Laye Claude Debussy was born in 1862.   To the north of the château lies the parterre designed by Le Nôtre in 1676, although subsequently much modified, ending on a magnificent terrace which is a mile and a half long. From here, in the opinion of the homesick James II, as superb a view could be enjoyed as that from the terrace at Richmond.

Between St. Germain and Paris lies the fascinating château of Malmaison.   The low and simple exterior has few architectural pretensions, but the interior contains a Napoleonic museum of the greatest interest to students of that period.   The house was bought by the future Empress Josephine when her husband was First Consul, and here she held her literary *salon* in jealous imitation of Madame Récamier and Madame de Staël.   After her divorce in 1809, Josephine retired to Malmaison and solaced her loneliness in her garden and conservatories. In the former there still grow some varieties of the roses which were her particular pride, while in the latter she grew the "Malmaisons" destined to keep fresh the memory of her beautiful home.   It was here in 1814 that the Empress, doubtless with rather mixed feelings, received the congratulations of the Allied sovereigns after Napoleon's abdication. The coolness of the weather and perhaps the emotional strain on that occasion proved fatal to Josephine's health, and she died shortly after in the handsome mahogany bed, ornamented with ormolu, which can still be seen in the Empress's bedroom.

A few miles south of Malmaison is situated the Park of St. Cloud, which covers the hill-slopes and the plateau between Garches and Ville-d'Avray.   The park still retains some of its original lay-out, and the Grande Allée makes an imposing approach to the beautiful Grande Cascade, a massive fountain consisting of a higher and lower portion by Le Pautre and Mansard respectively.   In the gardens which occupy the position of the château the visitor may pause to speculate on the beautiful building, with its great historical associations, which once stood on this site.   Originally built in 1572 by Charles IX, his brother the effeminate Henri III was murdered there by a crazy monk seventeen years later.   In 1658 St. Cloud was entirely rebuilt according to the plans of Mansard, and here in 1670 died "Minette," the English wife of Philippe d'Orléans and the beloved daughter of Charles I.   The fall of the Directory was encompassed by the First Consul at St. Cloud, where in 1810 he was married to his second wife, Marie-Louise of Austria. In 1870 the château witnessed a melancholy scene, when the disease-ridden Napoleon III left the threshold for the calamitous war destined to extinguish his Empire and during which, as the result of bombard-ment, the beautiful and historic building was burnt to the ground.

On the south side of the Park of St. Cloud lies the old town of Sèvres, celebrated for its porcelain factory since 1758, when the brothers Dubois transported thence their works from Vincennes.   At first only an artificial porcelain called *pâte tendre* was made, producing the *Vieux-Sèvres*, but after the discovery of china-clay near Limoges in 1769 the manufacture of hard porcelain, or *pâte dure*, facilitated the creation of much larger figures and vases than was possible with the *pâte tendre*.   In 1760 the factory was purchased by the Crown, and the royal interest taken in it, particularly by Louis XV, is reflected in the names *bleu de Roy*, *rose du Barry*, and *rose Pompadour*.   In the Manufacture Nationale de Sèvres, as it is officially known, was arranged that most unlucky and short-lived treaty between Turkey and the Allies.   But it had at least the rare distinction of being signed in a factory of porcelain which is as renowned and beautiful as any in Europe.

Passing through Argenteuil, famous for its vineyards, asparagus, and, in the hideous Second Empire church, the supposed "Seamless Garment of Christ," Ecouen, due north of Paris, is reached.   The Renaissance château here is one of Jean Bullant's masterpieces.   Built about 1530, it is the prototype of the Petit Château at Chantilly, and both were constructed for the same patron, Constable Anne de Montmorency. Chantilly, north of Ecouen, is of artistic importance, although the Grand Château, as apart from Bullant's erection, was built in the second quarter of the last century.   This large château, which is beautifully situated in the middle of a lake, now houses the Musée Condé, con-taining the most important collection of pictures within easy reach of Paris.   The original Grand Château was built by Mansard for the Grand Condé, and inspired Lord Herbert of Cherbury to remark that "it was an incomparable residence, admired by the greatest Princes of Europe."   Unluckily, it was burnt at the Revolution, and the Duc d'Aumale, the heir of the last of the Condés, was responsible for the present erection.   Although the duke suffered banishment both under the Second Empire and the Third Republic, he most magnanimously bequeathed his whole domain to the Institût de France. Apart from historical and artistic connections, Chantilly should be of peculiar interest to cooks, since here the famous chef Vatel, on realising that the fish course was late for Louis XIV's dinner, instantly took his own life.

Some distance south-east of Chantilly lies the interesting town of Meaux, built round a loop of the Marne, which is the centre of the fertile "Pays Meldois," so called from the Meldi, a Gallic tribe which once occupied the surrounding territory. The chief interest of Meaux, besides the delightful old mills of timber and brick dating from the sixteenth century, is the Cathedral of St. Stephen, which is a weather-beaten and picturesque building erected from the twelfth to the sixteenth centuries. The beautiful south portal is similar in period and architecture to that of Nôtre Dame in Paris. The interior, which is pleasing except for the stumpy nave, contains the tomb of the great preacher Bossuet, who honoured Meaux with his residence as bishop for the last twenty years of the seventeenth century.

The road from Meaux to Melun, which lies almost due south of Paris, passes through the lush pastoral country of the Plateau de Brie, famous for its delicious cheeses. Brie-Comte-Robert, a town less pretty than its name suggests, is the centre of the industry, and its church contains a superb rose window in the apse of the thirteenth century. As a contrast to cheese, beer is brewed in the neighbourhood, and Crisy-Suisnes is a rose-growing centre. Melun is the capital of the department of Seine-et-Marne, and it is to be hoped that the incidence of its mention in Julius Cæsar's *De Bello Gallico* as Melodunum may somewhat atone for its singularly unprepossessing appearance to-day.

A few miles south lies Fontainebleau, which, after Versailles, is the most interesting and best-known royal palace in France. For these reasons its superb architectural and artistic treasures are too resplendent for these pages, although it may be relevant to the consideration of the Île-de-France to mention a few of Fontainebleau's historical connections. When only a fortress existed where the palace now stands, Thomas à Becket in 1169 took refuge in it from the hasty temper of his royal master, and here from the twelfth to the fourteenth centuries four kings of the House of Capet were born and two died. The real creator of Fontainebleau however, was François 1er, who formed there the brilliant "School of Fontainebleau" with the artists he had imported from Italy. Henri IV further embellished the palace at great cost, and here in 1601 his son, later Louis XIII, was born. Amongst many distinguished foreign visitors can be numbered that eccentric convert to

Catholicism Christina of Sweden, Peter the Great, and Pius VII, who was compelled to renounce his temporal sovereignty in the palace by Napoleon. The Emperor, indeed, made Fontainebleau his principal residence, and spent twelve million francs on its restoration. Here he signed his abdication in 1814 and took his touching farewell of the Old Guard in the Cour du Cheval-Blanc. His nephew Napoleon III usually spent a month or more of the summer at Fontainebleau, and there is a delightful photograph of the crinolined ladies of the imperial court in the early 'sixties grouped on the steps of the "Étang de Carpes" and gazing down in admiration on the top-hatted Emperor and the juvenile Prince Imperial, who are posed together in a small canoe.

Having completed the first and smaller circle of the environs of Paris, a wider one will now be drawn to include other places of interest in the Île-de-France more remote from the capital and in the contiguous departments of the Loiret and the Eure-et-Loir. Orléans is the capital of the Loiret, and apart from the cathedral, which is mentioned later, the town itself is of great historic and some artistic importance. The connection of Orléans with the famous family of that name dates from 1344, when it was made the capital of a duchy and given to a younger son of Philip VI. On three later occasions it was conferred on cadet branches of the royal family, and from Philippe d'Orléans, for whom the last creation was made, was descended the regicide Philippe Égalité and his more amiable son Louis-Philippe, later King of the French. Those desirous of being reminded of the military reverses inflicted on the English by Joan of Arc should visit Orléans on May 8th, when appropriate celebrations are held to commemorate the final ejection of the enemy in 1429. Orléans was the scene of many excesses during its later history. It was sacked by the Calvinists and later became their headquarters during the Wars of Religion; it suffered the bloodthirsty dictatorship of Barère during the Revolution; and in 1870 it was occupied for three months by the Prussians.

Orléans is an attractive town with many wide eighteenth-century streets and squares in an architecture inspired by Paris. From the Pont Georges V, which crosses the Loire, a delightful view of the general lay-out of the city can be enjoyed. There are two museums of some interest in Orléans: the Musée Fourché and that housed in the old Hôtel de Ville. The Fourché, which contains a formidable collection of rather undistinguished canvases, miniatures, and ivories, was presented to the town by the late Monsieur Fourché. The delightful works, however, of a lesser known painter of the early nineteenth century called Coignet, an artist in the fashion-plate genre, enliven the general level of mediocrity. This artist's work is similar in technique

72 (*opposite*)   The Buttresses of Chartres
73, 74, 75 (*overleaf*)
Cathedral Sculpture at Bourges, Chartres, and Amiens

76, 77 Portals and Towers of Chartres

and subject-matter to that of the inimitable Boilly.   The old Hôtel de Ville, built about 1500, is a graceful example of the *flamboyant* style, and houses a great mass of pictures many of which would look charming in a private house but lose their point in a museum.   There is also, of course, a Musée Jeanne d'Arc.

The Loire descends southwards from Orléans through gently undulating country renowned for its game and the pike which form the delicious "Quenelles de Brochet," until Gien is reached on the border of the old provinces of Orléanais and Berry.   This is a delightful little town, situated on the right bank of the river, and after a lunch, which at Gien is certain to be memorable, the visitor may feel constrained to mount to the late-gothic château which dominates the place, where he can enjoy a magnificent view of the valley of the Loire.

The country in the Loiret, although mainly flat, is more interesting than that in the Eure-et-Loir, which lies to the north-west, and where most of the scenery is sadly reminiscent of the northern plains of France.   In the neighbourhood of Châteaudun are grown large fruit and mushroom crops, and the great expanse of arable land stretching northwards to Chartres provides excellent partridge shooting.   The massive château, which belongs to the Duc de Luynes, at Châteaudun is most impressively situated on a promontory above the Loir, and the *donjon* is said to date from the late tenth century.   The *corps de logis*, with its truly magnificent *flamboyant* stairway, was built in 1464 by the intrepid soldier Jean Dunois, the "Bastard of Orléans."   The fortunate public is allowed access to this beautiful château.

Passing through Chartres, where the interest is naturally concentrated in the world-famous cathedral mentioned later in this section, Dreux is reached in the Île-de-France.   It is a town noted for the tombs of the House of Orléans in the Chapelle Royale-St. Louis. Undoubtedly these are of a period rather than of an artistic importance, but there is much pathos and unconscious humour in this great array of tombs and monuments which King Louis-Philippe began to erect during his reign.   The recumbent figure of the Duc de Penthièvre, who died as a child, is a delightful work of James Pradier, better known for his less successful work on the "Fontaine Molière" in Paris.   The life-size statues of the king and his queen, Marie-Amélie, which stand in front of the High Altar, are both in volume and conception typical of the pseudo-grandeur of the period.   Louis-Philippe stands erect in knee-breeches, a double-breasted tail-coat, and a long robe, looking towards the altar with an almost truculent gaze, while his wife, more devout, is kneeling by his side, her head bent in prayer.   Even more fascinating, perhaps, are the tombs of the Duke and Duchess of

Orléans, which, although contiguous, are separated by an open gothic grille, since the Duchess, being a Protestant, was buried just outside the consecrated precincts of the chapel. Her hand, however, stretches through this architectural barrier towards the recumbent form of her husband, as if in mute protest against the invidious segregation.

Continuing on the outer circle of the Île-de-France, Mantes is reached, situated due west of Paris. Owing to its charming position on the left bank of the Seine, this unpretentious little town has earned the sobriquet of "Mantes la Jolie." It was burnt to the ground by William the Conqueror in 1087, but enjoyed a fitting revenge on that corpulent monarch, since his careless horse, treading on a cinder amongst the smouldering ruins, gave him the fall from which he subsequently died. Passing through Pontoise, on the Oise, which is renowned for its crayfish and cherries, Senlis lies on the right bank of the Nonette, surrounded by beautiful forests. It is a town of great charm which has suffered considerably at the hands of English watercolourists. For this mischance, however, it is entirely to blame, since Senlis abounds in many buildings which are indubitably picturesque. The cathedral, which is one of the smallest in France, is a gem of early thirteenth-century gothic. The spire in particular is of the greatest beauty, and unsurpassed in lightness and elegance for its period. It is perforated by high dormers crowned by gables leaning slightly forward which are reminiscent of the "mitre" hats worn by the stalwart grenadiers in Frederick the Great's army.

North of Senlis lies Compiègne on the Oise, with its great classical palace, which was the favourite residence of Napoleon I. The original château was of mediæval origin, but was entirely rebuilt by Jacques-Ange Gabriel and his talented family. Begun by him in 1755 and restored by Napoleon, Compiègne was considered by many critics of the last century to be a typical example of French "neo-classical decadence"; but to-day it is more justly appreciated as a building imposing for its mass effects and architectural sobriety. From the terrace there is a magnificent view of the thickly wooded park, which is pierced by a single broad avenue stretching to Beaux-Monts. This simple but impressive example of landscape gardening was carried out by the orders of Napoleon. The Petit Parc, which lies just below the terrace, consists of the usual formal garden with statuary and a trellis walk on the north side designed for the pleasure of the homesick Empress Marie-Louise, in imitation of her favourite promenade at Schönbrunn.

The interior of the palace, besides housing a fine collection of

Gobelin and Aubusson tapestries, also includes several suites with the original Empire furniture. Of these, the most impressive is the Galerie des Fêtes, decorated in white and gold and containing two rather grandiose statues of Madame Laetitia Bonaparte and her son the Emperor, in Roman costume. The state apartments are less happily conceived, being in the Second Empire style. But nearby are the rooms occupied by the Prince Imperial, with a delightful statue of Napoleon III's only child with his favourite dog, and also an exquisite set of table ornaments in the Balmoral tartan presented to that ill-fated prince, as may be surmised, by Queen Victoria.

Having concluded this arbitrary survey of the most important towns and domestic buildings in the Île-de-France, some reference must now be made to the cathedrals in this province, which, together with its contiguous departments, contains the majority of the finest ecclesiastical buildings in France. These will be grouped under three headings: those cathedrals roughly north of Paris; Nôtre Dame in Paris; and those approximately south of the capital.

Although this is not the place for a disquisition on French gothic art, a few points of general and particular interest should be borne in mind when visiting these beautiful erections. Gothic art, which originated in France early in the twelfth century, was contemporary with one of the most remarkable religious and artistic ebullitions of modern history. The essence of the first was concentrated in the spiritual revival effected through St. Francis of Assisi and his followers; while in the realm of the arts architecture, which predominated, was formulated and diffused through northern Europe by the genius and vigour of the monastic orders, of which the Benedictines led in brilliance and ability. To pass from the general to the particular, French gothic cathedrals, with a few notable exceptions, were built on a similar plan: the Latin cross is the foundation, with a *chevet*, or apsidal sanctuary surrounded by an ambulatory, from which radiate a varying number of side-chapels. It was indeed on the apse that the greatest ingenuity was shown, and it is in the cathedrals of the Île-de-France, and its contiguous provinces, that this beautiful design can be enjoyed to the best advantage. The exterior views of the apses of Soissons, Troyes, Bourges, and, in particular, Amiens show the acme of structural perfection in the gothic architecture of France.

The most easterly of the northern group of cathedrals is that of Châlons-sur-Marne. St. Etienne is not outstanding in merit in comparison with others, but it possesses an attractive and unusual exterior, since the main body of the building, which is in the late-thirteenth-century gothic manner, terminates on the west with a severe classical façade erected during the reign of Louis XIII. The interior of the cathedral, which is quiet and dignified, was originally built in the German manner, with an aisleless apse and choir, but this foreign plan was corrected during the fourteenth century by piercing the walls below the clerestory with arches and building three chapels between the buttresses. The great series of early sixteenth-century windows, which dominate the light in the nave, are remarkable for their variety of somewhat crude colouring and their affinity with pre-Raphaelite art.

Rheims, the next in the group of northern cathedrals, is famous for its agelong connection with the royal house and also for its phœnix-like resurrection from the ashes of the Great War. It was built during the course of the thirteenth century, in the flood-tide of gothic architecture, and the western façade, with its wealth of statuary, is a masterpiece of the period. What damage there is here was perpetrated by French revolutionaries rather than by German gunners. Although irreparable harm was done to the roof and the south-west front and a great quantity of stained glass was destroyed, the Germans were clearly not intent on completely demolishing the cathedral, as was so often asserted during the war, since they had every opportunity of doing this had they so desired.

The first view of the restored interior must inevitably be rather a shock, but a further inspection of the work recently completed should inspire the greatest respect for the eminent architect concerned, Monsieur Henri Deneux. In particular, the appearance of age given to the vaulting of the nave compares most favourably with nearly all nineteenth-century restorations. The grim interior of Angoulême springs instantly to the mind in contrast, and it is terrifying to speculate what the new Rheims would have resembled had Monsieur Viollet-le-Duc been alive to restore it.

The Archbishopric of Rheims was founded according to tradition by St. Sixte, said to have been consecrated by St. Peter himself and martyred under Nero. Here Clovis was baptised by St. Remigius in the fifth century, and all the Kings of France, with a few exceptions, were crowned in the cathedral, from Philippe-Auguste in 1180 to Charles X in 1825. The sacred ampulla from which they were anointed was destroyed by the mob in 1793. It was a vessel containing heavenly oil, said to have been brought by a dove for the coronation of Clovis.

Amiens, the most northerly of the great cathedrals, is said to be the third largest church in Europe, and it is certainly the biggest in France. In general style the cathedral represents the zenith of thirteenth-century gothic, and in some minor features shows the first tendency towards the *flamboyant*. The western façade is so encrusted with statues as to smother its design, but many of these are apparently of so improving a nature that they inspired Mr. Ruskin to write his *Bible of Amiens*. The immense size and homogeneity of the interior are most impressive, and are enhanced by the great height of the nave in proportion to its width and the general architectural simplicity. Apart from the rose windows, however, the cathedral suffers from an inadequate profusion of stained glass. The most notable part of the interior is the choir, raised six inches above the nave and approached by an eighteenth-century iron gate of great elegance and quality. The stalls, a hundred and ten in number, are richly carved and, for their period, the early sixteenth century, as fine as any in France. The choir screen in the ambulatory, with its gilded stone reliefs, offers a mine of information to the student of early Renaissance costume. Although Amiens suffered considerably at the frigid hands of Monsieur Viollet-le-Duc, it was remarkably lucky during the war to be spared the fate of Rheims cathedral. Nine shells, however, struck it at different times, and the roof was pierced on several occasions.

Beauvais is the most easterly of the cathedrals approximately north of Paris. St. Pierre, which was begun in 1227, owing to the absence of a nave coupled with its immense height, gives the most startling impression of any cathedral in France. Had the nave been completed on the original plan, this would have been the largest gothic church in the world. "Amiens is a giant in repose," wrote a Cambridge professor a hundred years ago; "Beauvais a tall man on tip-toe." Monsieur Huysmans evidently did not appreciate the superb lines of this cathedral, and described Beauvais as a "melancholy fragment, having no more than a head and arms flung out in despair, like an appeal for ever ignored by Heaven."

The impression of height in the interior is almost overpowering, but, considering that St. Pierre is one hundred and sixty feet high and only two hundred and thirty feet long, that is not surprising. Apart from the magnificent Beauvais tapestries on the walls, the cathedral is outstanding for its choir, the highest in existence, and for the beauty of the narrow arches formed by the twelve double flying buttresses which support the vault. The height of the choir at Beauvais has been a source of pleasurable bewilderment throughout the centuries and even succeeded in making a favourable impression on Mr. Ruskin. "There are few rocks even among the Alps," wrote the sage, perhaps a litttle irrelevantly, "that have a clear vertical fall as high as the choir of Beauvais." The failure to complete the nave is responsible for the survival of three bays of the old Carolingian nave, called the *Basse-*

Œuvre, a severely plain work, probably of the eighth century, which presents a drastic contrast to the towering gothic of the eastern limb.

For inspiration of design and variety of architecture the cathedral of Rouen, the last in this group, is perhaps without parallel in France. The *chevet* is, indeed, of quite outstanding beauty, since the ambulatory, in place of the usual solid surround of chapels, has the alternate bays empty: a plan which gives space and elegance. As the cathedral was begun in 1201 and not completed until 1530, the lover of gothic has in this church a unique field for the pursuit of his studies. The choir is perhaps the most important feature of the interior, being a pure example of the *rayonnant* style and containing some superb woodwork dating from the second half of the fifteenth century. Of the various tombs, the most striking are those of the Cardinals Amboise and of Louis de Brézé. The former, erected about 1520, is designed with a startling Renaissance exuberance; the Cardinals, although portrayed on their knees, would not appear to be seriously engaged in prayer. The florid tomb of Louis de Brézé, erected ten years later, has an unexpected adjunct in the kneeling figure of his widow, Diane de Poitiers, who was destined to spend her widowhood so well. The sentimental visitor will enjoy inspecting the mutilated figure of Richard Cœur-de-Lion in the ambulatory, and in recollecting that his heart is buried below.

The exterior of Rouen cathedral is too well-known to describe in detail, but the jumbled western façade, largely *flamboyant* and finished in 1530, never fails to cause amazement by its richness of detail and lack of design. The two towers of St. Romain and Le Beurre are probably the most famous erections of their kind in France. The former, which mainly dates from the end of the fifteenth century, has an ethereal and almost brittle appearance, and rises in superb contrast to the *flamboyant* tower of Le Beurre, with its sloping and secular roof. It is interesting to recollect that the strange name of this tower is not derived from its similarity to a pat of butter, but from the fact that it was built by the sale of indulgences granted for the eating of butter in Lent. The admirable result might seem to provide a specious argument in favour of these much abused pardons.

Having completed this short survey of the cathedrals north of Paris, it may be relevant to enter the capital itself in order to inspect Notre Dame. The first impression on arriving in the Place du Parvis is that Paris, in company with London, cannot boast to have built for itself either the largest or most beautiful metropolitan church in the country of which it is the capital. The west front, however, which is built in three storeys, is, for a gothic building, almost startling for its homo-

78 (*opposite*)
Gothic Fabric at Rouen

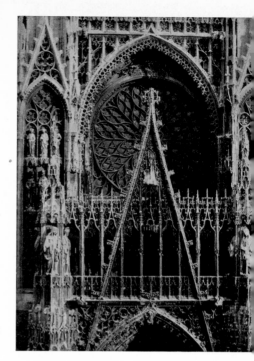

79   Rouen: a Detail of the West
Front

80   Amiens: the West Fro

geneity, and must have been erected from the designs of one very capable architect. The side façades and the apse have also this satisfying uniformity of style, being built in three distinct and receding elevations. The flying buttresses of the apse could not be excelled in boldness and beauty. The most famous ornamentations on the exterior of Notre Dame are probably the *chimères*, grotesque figures on the west side of the parapet, and it is interesting to speculate on the attitude of mind of the sculptor who could, for example, conceive those terrifying birds, half shrouded in drapery, which glare so viciously across Paris.

On entering the cathedral the visitor may be reminded of the aphorism of Mr. Edmund Sharpe, the mid-Victorian gothic revivalist, that in style Notre Dame was "the tomb of the Romanesque and the cradle of the gothic." It is, in fact, although much restored, the best example of transitional gothic in France. The thirteenth-century nave could not be excelled in grandeur or purity of style, although the transepts and ambulatory have unfortunately been defaced by the most inept frescoes of the last century. The triforium and clerestory are also noteworthy, since the circular windows between them, designed to give more light to the nave, are practically unknown in type outside the Île-de-France. The three great rose windows contain their original glass, although that in the west end was rearranged by Viollet-le-Duc. This architect must have thoroughly enjoyed himself in Notre Dame during the 'sixties, but his work here is more in conformity than usual with gothic inspiration. His pulpit, however, is hideous.

The history of Notre Dame has one remarkable connection with England, since in its choir in 1431 Henry VI was crowned King of France at the age of ten. A hundred and thirty years later in the same cathedral Mary Stuart was crowned Queen-Consort of Francis II. During the Revolution Notre Dame was, of course, desecrated, and another "queen" was crowned as Goddess of Reason. This lady was an opera singer, and she was attended for the ribald ceremony by a number of ballet dancers. After the restoration by Monsieur Viollet-le-Duc, Monseigneur Darboy consecrated the cathedral in 1864. It is curious to realise that nobody had ever thought of doing this before, and melancholy to reflect that the archbishop who pontificated at the ceremony was murdered seven years later in the Commune.

It is with some natural trepidation that the cathedral of Chartres, the first of the group south of Paris, is mentioned, since no words can do justice to its truly overwhelming beauty. Chartres should be approached from Maintenon on a fine summer's evening, when, driving

through the rich cornland of La Beauce, the great bulk of the cathedral
with its famous spires can be seen miles away, dominant and apparently
alone in this fertile countryside. Amidst the wealth of superb
sculpture which ornaments the exterior, the Portail Royal, which
pierces the western façade, is adorned with the most beautiful early
gothic statuary in France. These stylised figures, so reminiscent of
Byzantium, which fill the supports and the three tympana, are each
individually a work of genius; while in the placidity of their features
and the subtle elongation of their bodies they possess a quality of
almost ethereal spirituality lacking in the later achievements of realistic
art. Nevertheless, a word of mention is also perhaps worth while for
the sculptures of the stone screen enclosing the choir, mostly the
work of an unknown artist between 1525 and 1540. They are
theatrical in comparison with the grave majesty of the portal figures,
and accord none too well with their late-gothic setting, but the scenes
of domestic life and costume which they represent are often curiously
engaging.

On recovering from the overpowering effects of space and colour
on first entering the cathedral, two salient architectural features will
emerge. The first of these is the extreme simplicity, and even con-
ventionality, of the nave, completed, with the greater part of the
building, in 1260. The remarkable homogeneity of the structure will
next become apparent, since, with the exception of the entrance to the
baptistery, which has rounded arches, both the nave and choir are in the
same vigorous early-gothic style.

Of the incomparable stained glass which fills more than a hundred
and sixty windows it is only possible to mention those in the west
and the rose above them. The latter should be inspected from the
nave when the ingress of the evening light conceals the tracery and the
rose appears like a circular pattern of vivid colours set in a black
obscurity. Of the three windows below, yellow prevails in that on
the left, while the centre window is mainly a mixture of blue and
yellow; the right-hand window, which contains the Tree of Jesse, is
dominated by the most exquisite shade of blue. It would appear as if
the artist responsible for this superb display of graduated colour was
anxious to forestall or else to improve upon the uncertain beams of the
evening sun.

The interior of the cathedral, which has suffered so little from
nineteenth-century restorations, possesses, however, one unforgivable
blemish in the Assumption behind the High Altar, placed there in the
eighteenth century. It is almost inconceivable that such an incongruous and frivolous composition should be allowed to remain there

to-day.   In 1793, when the cathedral was being sacked by the liberated peasantry, it was indeed on the point of being destroyed when a resourceful curé placed a *bonnet rouge* on the head of the statue and succeeded in convincing the credulous rabble that, by his action, the Goddess of Reason had taken the place of the Mother of God.

The great interest of Ste. Croix at Orléans, the next cathedral eastwards of Chartres, is that, although it is an adequate example of the *rayonnant* style, it was entirely built early in the seventeenth century.   The original church was burnt by the Calvinists, and its reconstruction was begun by Henri IV in 1601 as a condition of his absolution by the Pope.   It was not completed, however, for over two hundred years, and during the eighteenth century Gabriel added the west façade, which in its gay, secular manner is the most satisfying part of the building.   The interior, although indeed correct, possesses no soul, and practically the only object of interest it contains is the lavish tomb of Monseigneur Dupanloup, that accommodating and able cleric who began his career as tutor to the Orléans princes and concluded it forty years later as the opponent of the promulgation of the doctrine of Papal Infallibility and the energetic defender of the privileges of the Church against the encroachments of the Third Republic.

There is a considerable contrast between the imitative frigidity of Orléans cathedral and the warm beauty of Bourges, which is the next of the cathedrals south of Paris.   Begun in 1192, this superb gothic pile was not completed until 1324.   There are two famous views of the exterior, one from the square facing the west façade and the other from the public gardens on the north side.   The former shows the two unequal and rather inelegant towers, with the five portals below which pierce the entrance front.   The very existence of five entrance doors indicates the immense width of the interior, although their statuary is later and inferior to that at Chartres.   The active and realistic figures, however, over the centre tympanum, participating in the Last Judgment, are very chastening.   A finer view of the cathedral can be obtained from the public gardens, where the apse rises with superb elegance in three divisions to the roof.   These are united with picturesque assurance by a profusion of flying buttresses.   The Hôtel de Ville in the left foreground, with its severe classical lines, completes a picture which even long familiarity can never impair.

It is impossible to describe in these pages the wealth and beauty of the stained-glass windows, particularly in the apse, which, although they are a little later than Chartres, do not appear so remote from the visitor, and therefore acquire a certain visual impression of tangibility. There are actually a hundred and forty-one of these magnificent windows, dating from the late twelfth to the early sixteenth century, and they contain over sixteen hundred figures. The outstanding architectural features are the absence of transepts and the double aisles to the nave, choir, and apse. Bourges is the only French cathedral, save Notre Dame in Paris, which is planned on this exceptional scale.

St. Etienne at Sens, the last of the cathedrals to be mentioned in this section, is of particular interest to the English owing to its connection with St. Thomas à Becket and the fact that William of Sens, the master mason of St. Etienne, was probably responsible for the erection of the east end of Canterbury cathedral. The exterior of Sens, which, begun in 1130, is the earliest Transitional building in France, has suffered mutilation through the centuries at the hands of the weather, the mob, and Monsieur Viollet-le-Duc. The sculptures of the central doorway are, however, fine twelfth-century work. On entering the cathedral, it will at once be realised that Sens might be the parent of Canterbury; particularly on inspecting the east end, where the termination of the five-sided apse, with arches rising from transversely coupled columns, is a feature largely identical in both buildings. The pure Transitional nave was roughly handled by Monsieur Viollet-le-Duc, who also destroyed the middle-pointed chapels in the aisles and substituted for them the miserable caverns which unluckily still exist. Fortunately, however, the beautiful *flamboyant* transepts were spared, together with the majestic baldachino designed by Servandoni in the middle of the eighteenth century. The gothic and classical in the sanctuary blend most happily together.

In the treasury are preserved the chasuble and mitre of St. Thomas à Becket, who visited Sens in 1164 to consult with the Pope on the attitude to be adopted towards the King of England. After the murder of the saint these vestments were preserved with great veneration, and it is said that after that time no one ever wore them with the exception of Cardinal Manning, who, seven hundred years later, playfully tried them on when visiting Sens cathedral.

81   The Garden, Château de Maintenon

82   Bourges: the Apsidal *Chevet*

CHAPTER VI

BURGUNDY AND THE CENTRAL PLATEAU

THERE is no district of France which suggests by its name such a picture of plenty and prosperity as Burgundy; it immediately conjures up a vision of fine wine, good food, and a rich countryside of rolling, vine-clad hills. The picture is essentially correct, and Burgundy shares with Perigord the distinction of first place amongst the gastronomic districts of France.

Thus to the greedy the appeal of this part of France is principally material, but to the antiquarian its interest lies rather in the romance of its early history, when for several centuries the Dukes of Burgundy rivalled in power and influence the Kings of France, and equalled, if they did not exceed them, in territorial possessions.

The rulers of Burgundy sprang from the same stock as the French kings, since early in the eleventh century Henri I of France had given the duchy, which stretched from the Jura to the Saône and included the province of Franche-Comté, to his brother Robert. This line of Capet dukes lasted until 1361, when the province reverted once more to the French crown under John II, who gave it to his son Philip, later named the Bold; thus begun the second Capet line, under which, during the fourteenth and fifteenth centuries, the province reached its most powerful phase by the acquisition of lands in Flanders and Brabant.

On the death of Charles the Bold in 1477, Louis XI, on the grounds of cousinship, claimed the whole of his dominions; but a fierce and partially successful opposition was raised by Maximilian of Austria, who hastened to the assistance of the harassed heiress, Mary, and greatly strengthened his position by prudently marrying her. The ensuing altercation was settled in 1482 by the Treaty of Arras, whereby Burgundy was confirmed to Louis, but the remainder of the possessions passed to Maximilian and later, through the marriage of his son to the daughter of Ferdinand and Isabella, to Spain. Thus, through the initial lack of diplomacy of Louis XI, the House of Austria was estab-lished in the Low Countries, which led to centuries of trouble for France.

In 1682 the title of dukedom of Burgundy was revived by Louis XIV for his grandson, the father of Louis XV, but this indicated no intensive

83 (*opposite*)
This name makes news

control, and from the sixteenth to the eighteenth centuries the country maintained a considerable measure of independence; it had its own assembly at Dijon, under a triumvirate consisting of the governor of the province, the Bishop of Autun, and the Mayor of Dijon, which was responsible for the area stretching from Champagne in the north to Lyonnais in the south, with Franche-Comté and Bourbonnais respectively to the east and west.

The landscape of Burgundy is on the whole gentle and domestic; it has none of the wild beauty of the central plateau which adjoins it on the south-west or the picturesque mountains of the Jura on the east. The monotonous plain which surrounds Paris rises gradually to a long, wide chain of hills which runs from north to south, and forms the western half of the province—the Plateau de Langres, as the northern part of it is called, melting southward into the Côte d'Or, the range which gives its name to the department. On the east the hills descend quickly to the wide plain through which the Saône flows in a long sweep as it emerges from the adjoining district of Franche-Comté. Close to the foot of the hills lies the capital of Burgundy, Dijon, while on the slopes of the Côte d'Or for thirty miles south are crowded the precious vineyards whose produce has doubly justified the name of the golden hills on which they lie.

The drive through the district is like turning the pages of a wine list: Chambertin, Vougeot, Nuits St. Georges, Beaune, Pommard, Meursault, Montrachet, and many other names famous all the world over pass in bewildering rapidity. In some cases towns have given their names to wines, such as Beaune and Nuits St. Georges, but in many others the magic name appears on a signpost pointing to no more than a modest château surrounded by a few acres of vineyards.

The most interesting and in many ways the most lovely time to spend in Burgundy is at the grape harvest, the *vendange*, which usually occurs about the middle of September. Early autumn can be lovely everywhere, but nowhere do the days seem so golden or the country so ripe and mellow as amongst these fertile hills, so that the harvest, which is a most important event in the lives both of peasants and owners, is given an added beauty. For months before the daily weather has been watched with the greatest anxiety: if there is too little rain the grapes will not swell, if too much they may be spoilt by mildew and lose their flavour. But there is a worse possibility than either of these, a rare but not unknown disaster; a heavy hailstorm, even of short duration, may utterly ruin the crop and so wipe out in a few minutes the careful work of many months.

With these misfortunes safely avoided, the *vendange* becomes a jolly

84   The Vineyards of Clos-Vougeot

The *Vendange*
in Burgundy

86 A Wine Press,
Beaune

87 Wine-bibbers at
Beaune

event, little short of a village social function.   Families of parents and children, all in large straw hats to protect heads and necks from the blazing sun, move along the rows of vines snipping off the bunches of grapes to an unbroken accompaniment of chatter and laughter.   The picked fruit is thrown into baskets which are carried to deep open carts standing on the edge of the vineyard, and so taken in gleaming mounds to the presses.

"O fortunate Burgundy," cried Erasmus in a moment of unwonted but understandable enthusiasm, "whose breasts produce so good a milk."

It is hardly surprising that a country which produces fine wine should also be renowned for good food.   From Dijon to Beaune, across the uplands to Saulieu, Avallon, and Chablis, in the department of Yonne, is a district in which it may be unwise for the greedy to linger for more than a few days; it is exceedingly probable that every meal, whether eaten in a town or a village, will be of such proportions and quality as to be something of a test for foreign digestions.

No town could make a more suitable capital of Burgundy than Dijon; it has an air of dignity and consequence such as many larger towns do not possess, and, although it has considerable commercial interests, the central part, with its vast palace and imposing buildings, gives an impression of political rather than industrial importance.   It is most fitting that its best-known product should be mustard.   In every other shop-window are proudly displayed rows and pyramids of little pots, in every shade of brown, yellow, and green, containing the different flavours of this excellent condiment.

The palace of the Dukes of Burgundy, which forms the central point of the town, presents a splendid if slightly monotonous classical façade to the great courtyard which faces the street, and sucessfully conceals the modest remnants of the castle built by Philip the Bold in 1366. Philip's tomb, one of the finest products of Burgundian gothic, now stands in the *Salle des Gardes* with the rather later monuments to Jean Sans Peur and Margaret of Bavaria, his wife.   They were brought to this rather unsuitable situation from the Abbey of Champmol, and, having been severely damaged at the Revolution, were restored, with an inevitable loss of character, in 1827.

In the west wing of the palace Gabriel built, in 1736, a grand staircase which mounts in two easy flights of stone steps, with balustrades of fine ironwork, to a huge room, decorated with panels of carving in stone set between Doric pilasters, which is said to have been designed by Mansard.   The greater part of the palace, however, is given up to the picture-gallery and museum, which in size is the second in France, but

12

in quality must come far further down the scale, though the collection of Rhenish primitives is outstanding.

Burgundian gothic can be studied in the several large churches, but it is the domestic architecture which gives so individual a character to the town. The streets are lined with the handsome seventeenth-century façades of private houses, the majority of which, though varying in size, are built on the same plan. A tall archway, large enough to allow the passage of a carriage, and closed with elaborately carved doors, opens from the street into an inner courtyard, on the far side of which are the main apartments of the house; the flanks are given up to coach-houses and stables, and the range fronting the street to porters and servants. It is the typical French plan, and is to be found in the old streets of Paris on the left bank and in many provincial towns; it has never been bettered where space is no object.

On the whole, these fine Dijon houses have maintained their air of elegance and prosperity, but buildings which originally housed a single family now contain several. One of the unlucky exceptions is the Hôtel de Brosses in the Place Bossuet, which is disfiguringly divided into several offices. As a charming example of seventeenth-century architecture and also as the birthplace and home of the redoubtable President de Brosses, who is remembered for his successful altercation with Voltaire, it deserves a better fate.

Southward from Dijon the road runs parallel to the lower slopes of the Côte d'Or to Beaune, the little town containing the *hospice* which is doubly famous for its remarkable picture and for its vineyards. The Hospital was founded almost five hundred years ago, and in the main is so little altered that it still gives an accurate impression of a religious foundation of the fifteenth century. The main ward, *La Grande Salle des Malades*, is a hall about one hundred and thirty feet in length with a vaulted timber roof; from end to end runs a central passage between a double line of beds, each with its little table and pewter bowl. One important change, however, has been made: whereas now there is only one occupant to each bed, in the past two or three wretches were pressed into each. The end of the ward is divided off by a grille to form a chapel, an arrangement to which there is an almost exact English parallel in St. Mary's Hospital at Chichester, and over the altar originally hung the famous *retablo* by Roger van der Weyden representing the Last Judgment. The picture has now, however, been removed to a gallery in another part of the building, where it can be more clearly seen.

North-west of Beaune the country rises to the rolling pastoral landscape of the Plateau de Langres, and the department of the Côte d'Or gives way to the Yonne; further north the hills melt gradually away past Avallon to Auxerre and Sens in the valley of the river which gives its name to the department. Along this valley runs one of the main roads from Paris to the south, passing through Sens, with its remarkable gothic cathedral, which has a particular interest for the English since it was designed by William of Sens, who later worked at Canterbury cathedral. From Sens to Auxerre the road keeps close to the Yonne, crossing from the right to the left bank at Joigny; the river, broad and gentle, winds through lush meadows and past groves of tall, shimmering poplars which thrive in the deep wet soil of the valley.

Auxerre, standing high on two hills above the left bank of the Yonne, retains something of the formidable air it must have worn in earlier centuries, and although the fortifications have mostly disappeared, the tough grey stone buildings and narrow streets winding up the hill suggest a town built primarily for defence. Without possessing any outstanding buildings, it retains owing to its plan the romantic aspect of a mediæval town.

South of Auxerre, in the neighbourhood of Avallon, is one of the finest Romanesque churches in France, the Basilica of Vézelay. It stands in a superb position on a high, grassy hill which rises abruptly from the open plain through which run the Yonne and its tributary, the Cure; on the western side a little village straggles up towards the summit of the hill, but from all other aspects the magnificent building crowns the steep slopes uninterrupted by any adjacent erection. The reason for the foundation of the basilica on this spot was extremely controversial. As described in the chapter on Provence, the body of Mary Magdalen was transported at the time of her death to the church at St. Maximin, but, to the astonishment of the religious world, during the eleventh century it was suddenly announced by the monks who inhabited the modest abbey at Vézelay that they had in their possession the bones of the penitent. By what means they had acquired them was not disclosed, but in spite of protests from St. Maximin, pilgrims abandoned the Provençal church and flocked to Vézelay. With the immense amount of money produced by the pious the splendid basilica was built, and for several centuries entirely ousted St. Maximin as a place of pilgrimage. Thus St. Maximin retired into a reluctant and jealous obscurity until an enterprising monk was fortunate enough to unearth a skeleton which was declared to be that of the Magdalen, while the bones which had been purloined by the monks of Vézelay were said never to have been hers. This lucky find was accepted by the Church, and the northern rival was henceforward entirely discredited.

The basilica is now owned by the State, and has been restored with the usual soul-destroying thoroughness.

This rich and beautiful part of Burgundy was formerly a district of great estates surrounding houses of an appropriate magnificence. The estates have succumbed to the inevitable process of diminution, but the châteaux survive in varying conditions of repair. In the wide agricultural landscape of hills and woods, varied with occasional patches of precious vines in the neighbourhood of Chablis and Tonnerre, lie some of the finest châteaux in France. Ancy le Franc, the home of the Clermont Tonnerre family, for example, which was begun in 1546 from the designs of the Italian architect Sebastiano Serlio (1475–1554), is not only a magnificent house but is also particularly important in architectural history as being almost the earliest truly classical building in France; while a few miles to the north lies the splendid Château de Tanlay, which dates from various periods during the sixteenth and seventeenth centuries. Great avenues of approach, gatehouses, courtyards, bridges, and moats form a splendid architectural prelude to this extremely interesting house. Further south, in the region of Semur-en-Auxois, where low hills rise from the valley of the Armançon, stands the superb château of Bussy-Rabutin, dating principally from the reign of Louis XIII, which is now under the care of the Government, and Epoisses, in the lower country between Semur and Avallon, which is only the surviving half of a house, the remainder having been destroyed at the time of the Revolution.

Beyond the stream of the Serein the country rises to the Monts du Morvan, the rather bleak plateau on which stands Saulieu, a little town whose gastronomic reputation has eclipsed the interest of the Church of St. Andoche, the tall dark nave of which is a remarkable example of small-scale Burgundian Romanesque.

Between Burgundy and the frontiers of Switzerland lies the considerable province of Franche-Comté, extending from the plains of the Saône valley on the west to the mountainous country of the Juras on the east, and containing in its varied landscape some of the prettiest country in France. Historically the province is less closely united to Burgundy than its geographical situation would suggest. By the Treaty of Arras in 1482, which has already been described, Franche-Comté, which was part of the dominions of Charles the Bold, passed to Maximilian and so followed the history of the Low Countries for two centuries. Louis XIV, however, was determined to unite it to the crown of France, and, after repeated invasions, received it by the Treaty of Ninveguen in 1678.

Through the northern part of the province runs the river Doubs,

88   Dijon: the Ducal Palace

89   Dijon: a Renaissance Doorway

90   Lyons and the Rhône

91   The Wooded Valley of the Doubs

which, rising amongst the mountains of the Swiss Juras, cuts a deep cleft through the hills until it emerges into the plain and joins the Saône north of Châlon. The long, winding valley is extraordinarily beautiful: at times the steep wooded hills descend to the water's edge; at others the valley widens and the river flows between flowery meadows and small arable fields which mount in steps up the gentler slopes. Away to the east the country rises to the barrier of mountains which marks the frontier of Switzerland.

As the valley opens out, the river makes a bend so sharp that it almost returns upon itself; on the peninsula thus formed stands Besançon, the capital of the province. It is a site of great strategic strength, since the neck of the peninsula is barred by a precipitous hill which is defended by one of Vauban's geometrical forts. In a tunnel under the hill passes the canal which connects the Rhône with the Rhine. In spite of its apparently impregnable site, however, the town was captured and lost on several occasions by the French armies in the course of Louis XIV's attempts to obtain control over the province.

A great part of the town was rebuilt following the union with France, and Besançon has now a very similar aspect to Dijon, which is sixty miles away to the west. There are the same fine squares and streets lined by the stone façades of seventeenth and eighteenth-century houses; in some the houses back on to large gardens, so that from the archways on to the street one has a charming glimpse of tall trees beyond stone-paved courtyards. Of the eighteenth century buildings, the most beautiful is the Préfecture, which was begun in 1771 from the plans of Victor Louis, the architect of the Palais Royal in Paris and the theatre at Bordeaux. The grey stone façade to the forecourt, with a wide central pediment supported on pilasters, is particularly successful, while in the interior there is a magnificent oval reception room designed in the grandest Palladian manner, with long windows looking out upon a very shabby garden. Another most attractive building is the present house of the bishop close to the cathedral, in which a mediæval tower has been incorporated into the gayest little Louis XV structure. Other Renaissance buildings, such as the Hôtel de Ville and the Palais Granvelle, though robust, are not of the first order.

In a small square leading up to the cathedral, which is closed by a splendid Roman arch dating from the time of Antonius, is the birthplace of Victor Hugo, a little house which now shelters a *bistro* of his name; while in a house across the square were born the brothers Lumière, who, with singular propriety only perhaps exceeded by Mr. Bell and the telephone, invented the cinematograph.

13

The cathedral is a confused and unsatisfactory building, but the sacristy is outstanding for the beauty of its panelling and for the magnificent collection of vestments which it contains.

South of Besançon the country rises to a district of grass-covered hills and wide arable valleys watered by streams which, though usually shallow and gentle, become during the melting of the snows fierce and swollen torrents. Close to one of these streams, named *La Furieuse* owing to its intemperate spring behaviour, lies Salins-les-Bains, once famous as a watering-place, but now abandoned to the commercial production of salt. It still preserves a relic of its fashionable days in the beautiful town-hall, which was begun in 1718; the name of the architect appears to have been lost, but the charm of the design would suggest that it was the work of an artist such as Jacques Gabriel the Younger.

Between Salins and Champagnole, the little town on the river Ain famous for its food, is a wide, high country of good farming land. Here, as in Burgundy, the farmhouses, outbuildings, and yards are grouped together for protection and company during the long winter months when the country is under snow. It is a practical arrangement for a gregarious people which is found in many parts of France, but there is an obvious economic drawback in the great wastage of time entailed in bringing in the horses, cattle, and produce from distant fields. This custom accounts for the many herds of milking cows which obstruct the motorist at every turn of the road.

Regarded as villages, these conglomerations of buildings are rather squalid, but as farmyards they are distinctly picturesque. The great stone barns have wide, semicircular, arched doorways built large enough to take a well-laden farm cart. On the verges of the road lie heaps of manure, while all about the highway stray a comparatively road-minded crowd of chickens, pigs, guinea-fowl, geese, rabbits, and endless dogs. Cottage gardens full of flowers, sunflowers, and many-coloured dahlias, crimson vines trailing over stone farm-buildings, carts piled with green loads of the last hay-crop make up an autumn picture which must have remained unchanged for centuries.

A few miles west of Salins, on the borders of the plains, lies Arbois, the town where Pasteur lived and died; in this district are the vineyards producing the pleasantest wine of the Juras, the rich, golden Arbois, which has a delicious bouquet suggestive of spring flowers.

South of Champagnole the country rises slowly to the Juras. The wooded hills begin to encroach on the arable fields, and forests of beech and ash mingle their bright colouring of spring or autumn foliage with the sombre green of pines. On the higher ridges beyond the little towns of St. Laurent and Morez the deciduous trees disappear and thick groves of spruce, growing in broken drifts about the open, grassy slopes, give the landscape the appearance of a well-planted but essentially Victorian English park.

The tail of the province of Burgundy creeps round the southern extremity of the Franche-Comté and insinuates a strip of country, now part of the department of Ain, between it and the Swiss frontier. This district, which was secured for France by M. de Talleyrand at the Congress of Vienna, is subject to both Swiss and French customs regulations, but in spite of this dual control it is one of those happy places where all spirits, ranging from petrol to whisky, are sold without tax. The centre of it is Gex, a charming little town on the lower slopes of the Juras; from the terrace-like streets there is a magnificent view eastwards across the Lake of Geneva to the shining peaks of the Alps far away in the heart of Switzerland. Above Gex the road mounts steeply to the Col de la Faucille, and so passes into the Franche-Comté. A few miles away, in the village of Thoiry, took place in September, 1926, the once famous but now almost forgotten Franco-German conversations between M. Briand and Herr Stresemann.

The tail of Burgundy is the most picturesque part of the province. The river Ain, which rises within a few miles of the Doubs, is joined by the Serpentine, and the considerable river thus formed flows amongst the western slopes of the Juras and descends by rocky gorges and cascades, some of considerable height, towards the woods and fields of the plain of La Bresse. On the famous farms of this district is bred almost every chicken, if one is sufficiently credulous to believe one's menu, which is eaten in France. It is natural that the home of the best chickens should be a district of good food; the larger towns, such as Bourg-on-Bresse, contain a dazzling bevy of restaurants, at any of which one can obtain a meal never to be forgotten, but perhaps the most charming of these towns is Nantua, which has given its name to the *quenelle* made from the pike caught in the lake on the shores of which the town lies.

Between Burgundy and the Auvergne lies the little province of Lyonnais, consisting of the departments called after the two greatest rivers of France, Loire and Rhône; it is therefore perhaps fitting that the principal impression given by Lyons, the capital, is one of water. The town, which is the third largest in France, is situated in a deep valley at the junction of the Rhône and the Saône; the two rivers run parallel to each other through the town, in places approaching within a few hundred yards, at others coyly receding to a greater distance, and not eventually joining until they emerge amongst the southern suburbs.

The two rivers in the valley and the steep hills which rise from them have restricted the available space for building, so that the long

13*

peninsula on which stands the old part of the town has rather a crowded air: long, narrow streets run between tall buildings, squares are small, and churches and public buildings are closely hemmed in by their commercial neighbours. Beyond the Rhône lies the vast geometric modern quarter, laid out in a wide part of the valley; but where it narrows, houses are built picturesquely one above the other to the tops of the hills. During the disastrous landslides of recent years many of these houses descended, in sad confusion, one upon another, with a terrible consequent loss of life and property.

Like the majority of large towns, Lyons owes its birth to the Romans, who founded a colony here in 43 B.C. which they named Lugdunum; about a century later Augustus raised the colony to the status of capital of Celtic Gaul. After belonging successively to the Kingdom of Provence, the House of Straetlingen, and the Empire, it came to the French crown. The darkest period in the history of the town was during the Revolution, when, as a strong royalist centre, it was besieged by the army under Kelermann and surrendered after great bloodshed. As a punishment for this opposition, half the town was ordered to be destroyed, and it was not until the time of the Consulate that it recovered its former prosperity. Its growth into a town of major importance is due to the silk trade, which was begun as long ago as the thirteenth century. The first considerable encouragement to the industry was given by François 1er, who in 1536 gave two merchants of Lyons licence to set up looms for the "making of cloths of gold, silver, and silk." Similar advantages were given to other towns, such as Tours and Avignon, but through enterprise Lyons secured a virtual monopoly. Early in the nineteenth century mechanical looms were invented, so that the rich stuffs for which there was a heavy demand during the Empire were produced with greater economy and profit, and thus revived the trade which had been paralysed by the sentence of the Convention. The industry has now to compete against the productions of other countries, but for quality and design the silks of Lyons still maintain their unique position.

Although the silk trade is the most important enterprise, to the passing tourist, as well as to the resident, the excellence of the food is almost a rival. No town outside Paris contains such a string of restaurants, all so superb that it is difficult to make a choice. Will one dine in the heart of the town or in the little restaurant near the Parc de la Tête d'Or, where one sits at a table on the pavement of a quiet street and eats through a remarkable menu which does not vary, lunch and dinner, year in, year out ? Or perhaps patronise the famous restaurant on a terrace near the southern outskirts of the town, where,

The Wooded Hills of the
Puy-de-Dôme

A Valley in the Auvergne

94   An Upland Valley of the *Massif Central*   95   Milk for Roquefort Chee

from under pleached limes, one looks down on to the Saône flowing to its nearby union with the Rhône? Whatever the choice, the meal will undoubtedly be something to be remembered.

North of Lyons, to the west of the Saône, are the hills of Beaujolais, which give their name to the well-known wine which is grown on their slopes; the centre of the trade is Villefranche, through the long, sad street of which the main road passes to Mâcon and the North. Westward from Lyons stretches the vast central plateau of France, the great area of high ground which extends from the Rhône on the east to Limoges one hundred and sixty miles away on the west, and from the plains of Orléans in the north nearly two hundred miles to Carcassonne in the south. This plateau is roughly heart-shaped, with its point to the south, and has, in addition to its form, good reason to be looked on as the heart of the country, since amongst its hills and valleys rise almost all the rivers of France, with the exception of the Rhône, the Saône, and the Seine; thus it is the central fountain which gives life to the greater part of the country. The general formation is complicated; range on range of hills, rising here and there to the height of considerable mountains, run one into another in confused formation, but assuming principally a north-to-south direction. The highest point comes near the centre of this conglomeration at the Puy de Saucy in the Auvergne, which rises to nearly 6,000 feet, but it is closely rivalled by the Mont de Finiels in one of the ranges of the Cevennes, which is only a few hundred feet lower.

There is a strange air about this great central plateau which immediately isolates it from the surrounding plains; although geographically the heart of France, it is the only part of the country which seems essentially un-French. There are two main reasons for this: first the people, who are of Celtic origin and have somehow through the centuries maintained the characteristics of their race, and secondly the geological formation of the hills, which is the product of violent volcanic disturbances.

This upland country of wide pasturelands and fertile valleys is the home of a great store of tradition and legend, some founded on pagan origin, but the majority derived from the lives of the men who came to spread Christianity amongst the savage inhabitants. The stories of the saints who, in face of great opposition, founded religious cells in this remote part of Gaul are innumerable, and their names are perpetuated in the villages, the greater part of which are called after some saint whose history is long since forgotten. Nowhere in Europe outside Spain are to be found so many miraculous Madonnas, not only in towns such as Clermont Ferrand and Le Puy but also in small villages. Many of these wooden figures, of unknown age and blackened by time, have been objects of veneration for many centuries.

The great hero of the early history of the Auvergne was Vercingetorix, the champion of the Gallic peoples in their opposition to the invading Romans. He successfully defended the ancient capital, Gergovia, and almost destroyed the Roman legions under Julius Cæsar, but shortly after, in order to end the siege of the city of Aleria and save his troops from destruction, he gave himself up to the Romans. He was carried to Rome and compelled to walk in Cæsar's triumphal procession, and having served his purpose, was soon after executed, being then only twenty-six years old. Vercingetorix still remains a national hero to the Auvergnats, and his memory is suitably preserved in a large equestrian monument in the centre of the Place de Jaude, the main square of Clermont.

In the twelfth century part of the Auvergne passed to the English crown through the marriage of Eleanor of Aquitaine, who had been divorced by Louis VII, to Henry Plantagenet in 1152. Henry already held Normandy and Anjou, which he had inherited respectively from his mother and his father, and with this addition to his dominions he ruled over almost the whole of the western part of France. Eventually the Auvergne passed to the House of Valois and so descended to Marguerite de Valois, the final heiress of the family and the divorced wife of Henri IV; in 1610 she ceded the province to Louis XIII, Henri's son by her successor in his conjugal favours, Mary de Medici.

Following the destruction of Gergovia by the Romans, Clermont Ferrand became the capital of the province; in late years it has increased rapidly in size and importance owing to the vast Michelin tyre and other rubber factories which have sprung up on its outskirts. The heart of the town, however, retains its attractive but undistinguished air, and now, no more than in the seventeenth century, deserves Flechier's disparaging remark that "there is scarcely a town in France more disagreeable." The site even the most critical observer must find attractive; it stands on a steep slope with the great plain of La Limagne stretching away to the east, the plain of which Sidonius Apollinaris, Bishop of Clermont in the fifth century, wrote, "over a pastoral ocean, billows of precious harvest are tossing. The more a man travel across it, the more certain is he of escaping shipwreck, so gentle is it to voyagers, so fruitful to labourers, so generous to huntsmen." Behind the town rises the great bulk of the Puy-de-Dôme, reaching up to a height of nearly 5,000 feet. Flechier's principal objections to the town were the steepness and the narrowness of the streets; the steepness remains, but the streets have been greatly increased in width, thus adding to their convenience, but effectively robbing them of the attribute "quaint," which is supposed to be such an irresistible bait for the tourist.

The cathedral is a good example of thirteenth-century gothic, and is built on long, graceful lines, with fine glass in the windows of the choir; the pair of sprightly towers were added by Viollet-le-Duc. But the most interesting church in the town is Notre Dame du Port, a comparatively small Romanesque church dating from the eleventh century, with a crypt in which is kept a black Virgin which is the object of the greatest veneration to the Auvergnats. The façade of this church is exceedingly plain, but the grouping of the *chevet* of chapels at the east end, which mount up to an octagonal arcaded tower surmounted by a high conical roof, is particularly interesting in design. The outstanding feature of the interior are the capitals of the pillars of the ambulatory, which are elaborately carved with crowded groups of figures; they are rather clumsy in execution but intensely vigorous and lively in conception, and give a fairly accurate picture of customs and costumes of the early part of the twelfth century. The name of the sculptor, Robert, is carved on one of the pillars.

Close to the church, the walls of which must then have been slowly rising, Pope Urban II proclaimed the First Crusade to the assembled nobility of France in 1095. The impassioned words of Peter the Hermit stirred the crowd to the greatest enthusiasm, and many, it is said, passed into the crypt of Notre Dame du Port to consecrate their arms before the statue of the black Virgin.

The pure air in the district of Clermont is exceedingly bracing; in addition, the volcanic strata of the subsoil bring to the surface a great variety of hot and medicinal springs. These two advantages combine to make the northern part of the Auvergne the first health-resort district of France. Within thirty or forty miles of Clermont are to be found Vichy for the liver, Royat for the heart, Le Mont d'Or for the lungs, and La Bourboule for the throat, besides several others of lesser repute.

Southward from Clermont, towards Le Puy, the high, bleak plains of the *Massif* stretch away without a tree to break the monotonous prospect of endless grass and arable fields. Here and there a village clusters on a steep, volcanic hill below the ruined towers of a mediæval castle, while away to the west stretch the peaks of the Monts d'Or, which are often snow-capped for the greater part of the year. As in Burgundy, all farmhouses and buildings are crowded together in protective clusters, and so obtain a mutual support which must be essential during the hard winter months. In places the rigour of the landscape relaxes, as in the valley of the Allier, where groups of deciduous trees grow in the meadows by the twisting bed of the river, and in the neighbourhood of Le Puy, where the steep hillsides are clothed with dark woods of pine and spruce, while in sheltered corners are little orchards of apple-trees and a few plantations of walnuts.

Owing to the high altitude of the *Massif* the seasons are retarded almost a month behind those in the surrounding plains, and this is naturally most noticeable on coming from the south. One may leave Nîmes basking in the full beauty of early summer, while a hundred miles further north, on the plateau, the trees are still black and leafless, and even the birches, the first to break, show no more than reddening buds on their bare branches. The atmosphere also changes in quality; the deep, warm colour of the southern sky gives way to a clear, cold blue suggestive of frosts and icy winds.

The first sight of Le Puy from the surrounding hills is unforgettable: it is as if one were looking into a gigantic crater and seeing the lava atrophied into weird rigid forms. From the bottom of the valley rise three vast conical rocks round which the town is grouped; on one of these points stands the cathedral, on another towers a mammoth figure of the Virgin, made from the metal of two hundred and thirteen cannon taken at Sebastopol, while on the third, the most precipitous cone of the three, is the chapel of St. Michel d'Aiguille, which was built in this inaccessible position by Bishop Godescalk between the years 962 and 984. The top of the rock has been levelled, and from this platform rise the walls, enclosing roughly an oval in which pillars with richly carved capitals support the roof. The church is reached by a steep flight of over two hundred and fifty steps, the ascent of which on the knees was formerly considered a fairly chastening penance.

The construction of the cathedral is even more remarkable, since in this case the available level space was so restricted that in order to obtain sufficient length an arcaded porch was formed under the west end from which steps rise into the nave. The high façade necessitated by this arrangement, with its tiers of semicircular-topped arcades and windows, surmounted by three curious triangular gables, would be a fine example of twelfth-century design had not excessive restoration destroyed the texture of the stone. Before the present steps from porch to nave were formed in 1781, the long rise from the town was continued under the church and emerged in front of the choir; thus pilgrims making the ascent to the cathedral could have a distant view of the lighted altar while still far down the approach. Adjacent to the cathedral is a robust Romanesque cloister dating from the eleventh and twelfth centuries.

One may know that Le Puy is the capital of the department of Haute-Loire, but it seems so remote from the country one usually

96 (*opposite*)
The Rocher St. Michel at Le Puy

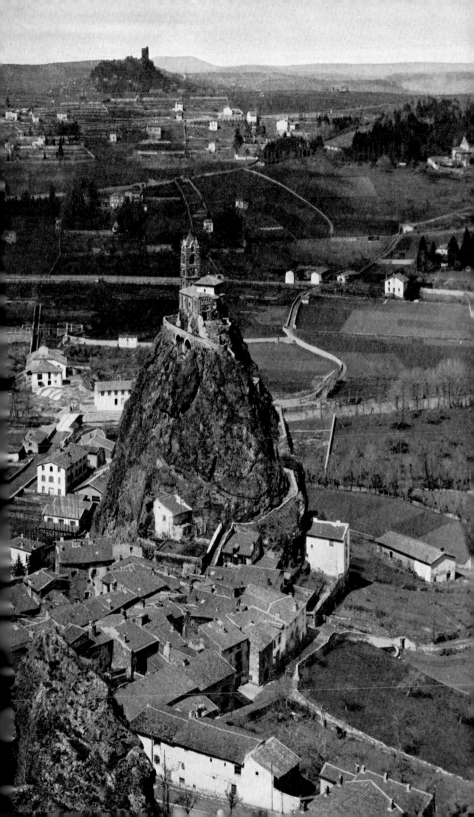

97　The Cathedr␣
of Albi

98　St. Flour: a Hilltop Town in the Auvergne

associates with the name of that river that it comes as a surprise to find
that it flows a mile or two to the east of the town. The longest river
in France is here still a stream of very moderate size, since it is only
twenty miles from its source in the Gerbier de Jonc.

West of Le Puy, beyond the valley of the Allier, rises the long range
of the Montagne de la Mageride, with the picturesque fortified town of
St. Flour amongst its further foothills. Further westward still the
landscape gradually loses its bleak upland air, although the towns, such
as Aurillac, retain a certain austerity; grass and arable fields alternate
with areas of forest, and steep slopes covered with beech and other
deciduous trees drop to the banks of swiftly flowing streams. As the
plateau breaks up into the valleys of the Lot, the Cère, and the Dordogne,
the gentle pastoral aspect increases, streams ripple through shady
meadows and wind amongst green hills, almost every one of which
appears to be crowned by a château, many in ruins but others still
inhabited. Amongst the latter Montal, near St. Céré, has an exceptionally beautiful François 1er façade to the courtyard, while the
Château de Castelnau, which is now the property of the State, occupies
a splendid position on a steep slope of hill overlooking the valley of the
Dordogne.

As the department of Lot gives way to Corrèze, the country becomes
even more beautiful. Crossing the Dordogne at the little town of
Beaulieu, squalid and dirty but with an interesting Romanesque church,
in the south porch of which is a magnificent tympanum, the hills
become more accentuated, though the scale remains small, and roads
wind desperately along slopes too steep for cultivation. Oak-trees
thrive on these hills, and sweet chestnut with their bright-green
foliage, and everywhere walnut-trees are cultivated, which are carefully
grown in large, formal plantations. To those who prefer domestic to
majestic scenery it may well seem the most lovely part of France.
Brive, on the Corrèze, the centre of this district, is an attractive, busy
town with a wide, shady boulevard forming a circle round the crowded
streets of the old quarter.

Passing southward and skirting the deserted foothills of the *Massif*
one comes to Cahors, built on an isthmus formed by a sharp bend of
the Lot; across the river as it turns northward strides the Pont
Valentré, an early fourteenth-century fortified bridge defended by three
towers which is said to be the finest of its period in existence. The
Romanesque cathedral on the other side of the isthmus is interesting;
the wide nave is covered by two flat domes, and in the tympanum over
the north door is an exceptionally fine Romanesque carving of the
figure of Christ. Cahors was the birthplace of Léon Gambetta, whose

memory is richly commemorated by a statue, a square, and a boulevard, and also of Pope John XXII, whose name is less carefully preserved. One hesitates to recall that the town was taken and sacked by English troops under the leadership of the Black Prince.

The south-western spur of the *Massif Central*, which is broken by the valley of the Lot, is a fertile country which clearly repays intensive cultivation and supports a large population. Agricultural prosperity does not, however, increase the beauty of the landscape, and it is not until one reaches the more barren hills round the sad, decayed town of Cordes that the country takes on a more romantic aspect. From Cordes the road rises over stony hills and drops gently to Albi in the wide valley of the Tarn.

This town has three principal attractions: its situation, its cathedral, and its pictures; beyond these there is little of great interest except a few small streets of old timber-framed houses and a large, well-planted square in which the inhabitants take their evening walk with almost Spanish enthusiasm. The main part of the town is built on the southern bank of the river Tarn, which here runs in a wide deep channel; a high bridge now crosses it to the north, but far below it still stands the Vieux Pont, which dates from the eleventh century and leads to the picturesque jumble of houses which mount steeply up the further bank.

The first sight of the cathedral is overwhelming. The great walls, built of a rose-pink brick, rise in a smooth sweep devoid of ornamentation to a parapet of battlements one hundred and twenty feet or so above the ground; at regular intervals these walls swell out into semi-circular bays in which loopholes command the flanking expanse of brickwork. The tower at the west end rises to twice the height of the walls, and resembles a keep rather than an ecclesiastical building. This remarkable example of the gothic style of the Midi was built during the century following 1280.

These austere defences contain an interior of startlingly contrasting elaboration. Every part of walls and roof is covered with early Renaissance frescoes of intricate patterns showing strong classical feeling, set against a background of deep blue, while round the choir is a remarkable stone screen carved with the luxuriant abandon of figures, niches, crockets, foliage, and so forth of the late gothic manner. Both the frescoes and the screen date from approximately the same period, 1500, but the former is the work of Italian artists, the latter of native French: comparison of the two styles thus forms an interesting study.

Between the cathedral and the river stands the former palace of the archbishops, a vast fortified building the greater part of which is more or less contemporary with the cathedral, and is also built of brick.

The interior was considerably remodelled during the seventeenth and eighteenth centuries, and the fortunate prelates who inhabited it enjoyed not only a house of supreme magnificence but also a lovely terraced garden laid out on the ramparts which descend to the Tarn. Two excellent galleries have now been formed in a wing of the palace to house the splendid collection of Toulouse-Lautrec pictures which was bequeathed to the town by the artist. At first sight it may seem somewhat strange to encounter these pictures, which represent principally the inhabitants of the lowest stratum of Parisian life towards the close of the last century, in what is a semi-religious building. On reflection, however, one realises the remarkable suitability, since no crusading archbishop could possibly produce a more biting and lasting denunciation of the vices of the *demimonde* than the satirical canvases of Toulouse-Lautrec.

For the greater part of its course the river Tarn passes through scenery of almost sensational beauty; the most famous stretch is above the town of Millau, where for a distance of nearly fifty miles it flows through a deep cañon which cuts through the wild limestone hills of the neighbourhood. The precipitous sides of the valley, which average 1,500 feet or more in height, sometimes approach to the water's edge, at others recede so that the river flows amongst narrow meadows lying below the towering cliffs.

The calcareous rocks of which the surrounding hills are formed are honeycombed with deep fissures and great subterranean caves, with often no more than the smallest exits to the surface. Narrow steps and passages lead far into the depth of the hills and open out into apparently infinite forests of dripping stalagmites and stalactites, whose creamy yellow formation assumes every kind of weird shape. To supplement the natural beauties, coloured lights are often installed, and, amidst gasps of surprise and delight from the cluster of visitors, the grotesque growths take on the vivid colours of the rainbow.

On either side of the valley of the Tarn stretch the strange barren hills known as the Causses, a name derived from the word *chaux* (limestone). No trees grow on these earthless uplands, which in many places have a surface of sheer, unbroken rock; but some of the lower slopes support a meagre covering of grass on which graze the ewes whose milk is used to make the famous cheese of Roquefort.

Crossing these derelict spaces, where there is no habitation in sight, one finds suddenly in a fold of the hills this little village, which sends its famous product all over Europe. In the cliff which rises steeply behind the single street are caves in the cold atmosphere of which the cheeses are kept until they have reached their highly pungent maturity.

CHAPTER VII

THE BISCAY COAST AND NORTHERN GASCONY

THE ancient province of Poitou stretched westwards from the picturesque valley of the Anglin, which lies east of Poitiers, to the Atlantic seaboard of the Vendée. It was bounded on the north by Anjou and Touraine and on the south by Aunis and Angumois. To-day that configuration is preserved by the three departments of the Vienne, the Deux Sèvres, and the Vendée, and its unity is emphasised by a scenic and historical similarity.

Poitiers, the capital, is the only town of importance in Poitou, and, apart from the two battles connected with its name, it is renowned for its ecclesiastical architecture. There are four outstanding churches in the city, including the cathedral, and of these the Baptistry of St. John takes precedence both in merit and age. This is probably the earliest Christian monument in France, and part of the floor and some of the arches date from the fourth and seventh centuries. The curious exterior is indeed more Roman than Romanesque. The baptistry is now used as a museum, and the exhibits should be of interest to the expert on the Merovingian era.

Far more striking to the eye than the simple lines of the baptistry is the luxuriant western façade of Notre Dame la Grande, which is adorned with more statues than any Romanesque church in France with the possible exception of St. Pierre at Angoulême. Built in the twelfth century, the façade is composed of three ranges of arcades surmounted by a gable, while on either side there is a group of columns, each supporting a "tourelle." The whole is encrusted with statues and bas-reliefs, bewildering both in number and variety. The complete lack of design, however, and the impossibility of distinguishing the individual statues make this façade an ingenious rather than a beautiful creation. In the interior, the barrel vault of the nave as well as the groined vaults of the aisles were shockingly disfigured by the crudest paintings in 1857.

The Church of Ste. Radegonde, dating from the eleventh to the fifteenth centuries, has also suffered from recent restoration, although the choir, built in 1099, and the "Angevin" nave, erected a few decades later, are both of great beauty. In the crypt is the ninth-century marble sarcophagus of Ste. Radegonde, blackened with age and emptied of its contents since 1562, when the remains of the patron saint of Poitiers were burnt by the Calvinists.   Some reparation was, however, made a hundred years later, when Anne of Austria erected round the saint's altar the present elegant balustrade.

A few steps from Ste. Radegonde lies the Cathedral of St. Pierre, begun by Queen Eleanor of England, who laid the foundation stone in 1162.   Although the exterior is rather commonplace, the carved wood choir stalls of the early thirteenth century are probably the oldest in France, while amongst a wealth of superb stained-glass windows the twelfth-century Crucifixion in the apse is outstanding, not only for artistic merit but also for the interesting fact that the features of Queen Eleanor and King Henry II are borne by two persons in the crowd at the foot of the Cross.

During the thirteenth and fourteenth centuries Poitiers often lay under English domination, finally returning to the French crown in 1369, when du Guesclin reconquered Poitou.   It is, however, curious that even to-day there remains a certain English flavour in the twisting streets and the grey stone houses, with their respectable and prosperous air.   The English must indeed have felt at home in this friendly city, situated in the midst of undulating and domestic scenery so reminiscent of their own countryside.

Near Nouaillé, which lies a little south of Poitiers, was fought the battle of that name in 1356 which re-established the power of England in Poitou and increased the reputation of the Black Prince.   More important, however, for Christendom was the first Battle of Poitiers, fought in 732, when Charles Martel defeated the Saracens, under Abd-er-Rahman, at a moment when they seemed destined to conquer western Europe.

A tour round the eastern boundary of Poitou from Nouaillé will bring the traveller to Montmorillon, rising prettily from either side of the Gartempe and renowned for the remarkable Octagon in the court-yard of the Maison Dieu.   This curious eleventh–twelfth-century erection consists of two chapels, one above the other, and once these were crowned with a pyramid and a funeral lanthorn.   The two latter incongruous objects have unfortunately disappeared.   North of Montmorillon lies St. Savin, which is notable for the unusually tall and crocketed spire of its abbey and the circle of Romanesque columns in the apse.   The eleventh-century frescoes, many of them life-size, are unique in France, but their beauty has been considerably impaired by the garish colours on the pillars which intersect them—the work of that all-too-conscientious restorer Viollet-le-Duc.

14

Châtellerault, north of St. Savin, which is renowned for the manufacture of arms and cutlery, is only of outside interest through its connection with the Dukes of Hamilton. In 1548 James Hamilton, the
Regent of Scotland, was given the dukedom of Châtellerault by
Henri II as an incentive to effect the marriage between the infant Queen
Mary of Scotland and the Dauphin Francis. Later, through failure in
the direct descent, the dukedom was forfeited to the French crown,
although the Hamiltons continued to claim it. Eventually it was
recreated by Napoleon III for the Duke of Hamilton of that period,
who had married a cousin of the Emperor. In consequence, the
dukedom of Châtellerault is one of the titles of the present Duke of
Hamilton.

North-west of Châtellerault lies Loudun, which possesses the inde-
finable charm of any town which once was prosperous and now is in
decay. Loudun suffered for its adhesion to Calvinism, and its prosperity was destroyed by the revocation of the Edict of Nantes. Its
population has gradually declined from twenty thousand in the seventeenth century to the four thousand at which it stands to-day. A
circular boulevard now surrounds the town where the ramparts once
stood, and the cobbled streets and tortuous alleys can only be traversed
on foot. The most remarkable monument in Loudun is the Church of
Ste. Croix, with its superb eleventh-century narthex and chancel.
This beautiful building has long since been desecrated, and its long
gothic nave is now used as a market-place. It is a strange and sad
experience, on entering at the west door, to gaze across the colourful
heaps of peppers, figs, egg-plants, and melons, which are a speciality of
the neighbourhood, to this derelict but pure example of Romanesque
architecture. Loudun is remote and it has no stars in the guidebooks,
but it is well worth visiting—except perhaps for the night.

In the contiguous department of the Deux Sèvres the principal town
is Niort, noted for the manufacture of angelica and for being the birthplace of Madame de Maintenon. North of Niort is the more picturesque town of Parthenay, which possesses two beautiful gateways
in the gothic Porte de l'Horloge, leading into the citadel quarter, and
in the earlier thirteenth-century Porte St. Jacques, a gaunt machicolated
erection at the entrance of the bridge over the river Thouet.

Two other towns deserve mention in the Deux Sèvres: Melle and
Lusignan. The former, lying in the valley of the Béronne, has three
fine Romanesque churches, of which St. Hilaire is the most notable for
its low apse and robust square tower. Lusignan also possesses a
beautiful eleventh–twelfth-century church in the priory of Notre
Dame, which has a triple nave of seven bays with cradle-vaulting; but

the town is more famous for having given its name to the illustrious family of kings who ruled over Cyprus from 1192 to 1489. The Lusignans were said to be descended from a water-fairy called Melusina, who possessed the rare power of being able to change herself into a serpent every Saturday. Misfortune, however, overtook her when she was detected by her husband in the process of this alarming trans-formation, and Melusina thereupon disappeared for ever, only being heard to hiss sadly for three consecutive nights whenever disaster threatened a member of the Lusignan family.

The Vendée, which is the most westerly portion of the old province of Poitou, was of course renowned for its devotion to the royal family during the French Revolution. The "Chouannerie," the name given to the peasant risings in Brittany and the Vendée, was finally crushed with great cruelty by General Hoche in 1795. The remote district of Bocage, where most of the fighting took place, is, as its name implies, a country rich in small copses, and the additional existence of hedges along most of the roads and bridlepaths was of great assistance to the rebels in their guerilla warfare. In 1832 the loyalty of the peasants in the Vendée was again proved when they rose in support of the Duchesse de Berry in her abortive attempt, on behalf of her son the Comte de Chambord, against Louis-Philippe, King of the French.

Roche-sur-Yon, the capital of the Vendée, lies on a plateau dominat-ing the valley of the Yon at the western extremity of the Bocage. The fact that Napoleon built it on a symmetrical plan in 1805 may give rise to pleasant expectations, doomed to disappointment on seeing the town. It is in reality a bleak, uninteresting place, in spite of the unusual regularity of its construction, and even the vast Place Napoléon, with its high classical church and the equestrian statue of Napoleon I in the middle, fails to impress the visitor. Roche-sur-Yon was com-pletely destroyed in 1794, during the "Chouannerie," and when the Emperor rebuilt it he renamed it "Napoléon," hoping thereby to ingratiate himself with the royalist inhabitants of the Vendée. Re-christened Bourton-Vendée at the Restoration, Napoleon III once again changed the name of this long-suffering town to Napoléon-Vendée, but it returned to its original and mediæval name of Roche-sur-Yon in 1871.

A short distance south-west lies the family bathing-resort of Sables d'Olonne, where on Sundays the fisherwomen still wear their *sabots*, their short black stiff skirts, and the white-winged caps known as *papillons*. The only other town of any size in the Vendée is Fontenay-le-Comte, pleasantly situated on both banks of the river Vendée, which possesses in the Château du Terre-Neuve a delightful Renaissance house

14*

built at the end of the sixteenth century. Approached by a long avenue and standing on a high plateau above the town, Terre-Neuve was originally the home of the poet Nicholas Rapin, and now belongs to the family of Rochebrune. It has a restrained classical entrance front, ornamented with five conventional statues, while the interior is delightfully furnished in different periods, ranging from the style of Henri IV to that of the Second Empire. When the family is absent it is usually possible for the public to enjoy this very typical example of a French country house.

The road from Fontenay-le-Comte to La Rochelle is flat and uninteresting, and midway Poitou is left for the ancient province of Aunis, which to-day forms part of the modern department of Charente-Inférieure. La Rochelle is one of the most picturesque and interesting of the smaller cities of France. During the Middle Ages it was held at different times by the English, who called it the "White City" owing to the reflection of lights on its sands and rocks. After the discovery of America, La Rochelle became one of the richest maritime towns in France. But the eager acceptance by the Rochelais of Calvinism diverted their attention from trade to religious warfare, and the revocation of the Edict of Nantes in 1685, followed in 1763 by the cession of Canada to England, destroyed the city's commercial prosperity.

La Rochelle falls easily into the two divisions of city and port, in the former of which the delightful arcaded streets dating from the sixteenth to the eighteenth centuries are an outstanding feature. Above these, in the rue du Palais, rises the Palace of Justice, a superb classical building completed in 1789. Its well-proportioned façade is ornamented with Corinthian columns. Nearby, in the same arcaded street, is the Hôtel de la Bourse, also built in the eighteenth century. It has a screen of simple columns facing the entrance to its unpretentious courtyard. Very different from these restrained and beautiful buildings is the *flamboyant* Hôtel de Ville begun in the reign of François Ier and finished in that of Henri IV. In the front court, which is entered through a battlemented curtain-wall, this ornate conglomeration of styles can be best studied, and many may be doubtful whether the oppressive arcade, with its coupled arches, is more hideous than the cumbersome dormers, writhing in pointless ornamentation, which pierce the steep roof above. This heavy façade is, however, enlivened by a classical pavilion, supporting a delicate belvedere, which unluckily contains a statue of Henri IV in enamelled faïence, perpetrated towards the close of the nineteenth century. The interior of the Hôtel de Ville was restored in the early days of the Third Republic.

A welcome change from the Hôtel de Ville is provided by the austere

99   Poitiers: a Detail of the West Front of Notre Dame la Grande

100   The Port of La
         Rochelle

101   Montauban : the Square

façade of the Cathedral of St. Louis, built between 1742 and 1784 on a gothic plan by the talented family of Gabriel.   The exterior is unfinished and, with the exception of a few columns with uncarved capitals, the entrance front is practically bare of any ornamentation whatsoever.   The interior, of which the ceiling of the apse is painted by Bouguereau in his gayest manner, is even more mundane than the majority of French eighteenth-century churches.

The old port of La Rochelle is extremely picturesque, since for several hundred years few boats larger than fishing-smacks have made use of its harbour.   The entrance to the quays is through the Tour de la Grosse Horloge, a gate which is worthy of its important function. The main structure, dating from the thirteenth century, is protected by two severe towers which, in fanciful contrast, are crowned with a group of eighteenth-century amorini upholding the celestial and terrestrial globes.   The body of the gateway is surmounted by a delicate classical cupola, and the whole construction shows the happy results of a fortuitous blending of the styles of the thirteenth and eighteenth centuries.   The sea entrance to this quiet port is protected by two sturdy mediæval towers, the larger, the Tour St. Nicholas, containing rather unexpectedly some finely vaulted rooms, including an oratory, approached by a double spiral staircase.   La Rochelle is altogether a delightful town, with the additional advantage of lying in a countryside rich in vineyards, which produce a brandy officially known as "Eau-de-Vie de Terroir."

Not far south of La Rochelle is Marennes, a name of significance to the gourmet through its association with a delicious breed of green oysters.   Marennes has some charming Renaissance houses and an imposing steeple of the fourteenth century.   It is neither easy to get to the island of Oléron, which lies opposite Marennes, nor indeed to leave it, since the ferry-boats are small, crowded, and spasmodic; and many think the island is hardly worth a visit.   The crossing, at least, is of considerable interest, particularly at low tide, when the oyster-beds become visible.   These are divided between the various owners by irregular rows of sticks, but it would not appear easy for the individual to recognise his own property in such a vast expanse of featureless mud. The transit from the mainland is made by the Pertuis de Maumusson, where the wide expanse of water is ornamented in mid-channel by the imposing Fort de Chapus, built by Louvois in the seventeenth century. It is to-day, of course, dismantled, and its beauty and isolation seem to demand a tenant of a romantic and anchoretic disposition.

Oléron is a flat and wooded island with a largely Protestant population, occupied with agriculture, vineyards, and the cultivation of oysters. In many places the pine-forests stretch down to a deserted shore. The chief town, Le Château, is undistinguished, except for the magnificent seventeenth-century ramparts overlooking the sea. At St. Pierre, in the centre of the island, is the only architectural monument of consequence on Oléron: the elegant thirteenth-century Lanterne des Morts, which is crowned with an eighteenth-century pyramid. It is a most unusual and becoming memorial to the dead. St. Pierre can also boast two further noteworthy possessions in the remains of Pierre Loti, buried in the back-garden of his former house, and in the clock-tower of the Church of St. Pierre, which may easily be the most hideous in France.

Royan, which lies on the mainland south of Oléron, is one of the most popular bathing-resorts on the west coast of France. It was once famous for the sardines (*royans*) which gave the town its name. The road thence to Mortagne skirts the northern bank of the Gironde, which is remarkable for the beauty of the little villages which lie by the edge of this great expanse of quiet water. Of these Talmont and St. Fort are exquisite examples. In the former the church sits precariously on a rocky promontory above the Gironde, while at St. Fort it nestles comfortably in a little group of plane-trees. Both these churches are typical of Saintongeais architecture in that the façades are strictly Romanesque, while the interiors, although planned in the same style, have gothic arches and ornamentation. Mortagne itself is uninteresting, but just outside lies the monolithic hermitage of St. Martial, originally hewn out of the rock by that saint and his companions about sixteen hundred years ago. At that time the sea approached to the foot of the high cliff, which must have increased the inaccessibility of this remote retreat. The chapel of the hermitage dates from the ninth century, and the tribune, reredos, and altar-rails are all hewn by hand out of the solid rock. The dark-green and shiny texture of the walls and roof produces an effect of gloom and asceticism which would have delighted the Romantics of the early nineteenth century.

The road from Mortagne to Jonzac leaves the bank of the Gironde and passes through the rich vineyards of the Saintonge, which produces the "Bons Bois," a brandy which is somewhat superior to that grown further north between Royan and La Rochelle. Jonzac has, in the main square, an imposing château of the fifteenth and sixteenth centuries, now used for municipal purposes. The great twin towers which flank the entrance are connected with the smaller *donjon* by a *corps de logis* which seems much restored. This robust entrance, however, gives an erroneous impression of the château's extent, since on the other side there is nothing but a group of amorphous buildings bisected by a public road. Facing the château on the opposite side of the square stands a machicolated gateway overgrown with pink valerian: a perfect subject for the female water-colourist of the Victorian era— to be painted, of course, in the afternoon light.

North of Jonzac the road to Saintes leads through the little-known town of Pons, with a large, rambling château of which the stately *donjon*, with Romanesque windows and high flat buttresses, dates from the twelfth century. Unfortunately the summit has been most meanly restored. The main square of the town is situated most unusually on a high plateau, and is surrounded by a pleasant public garden. The ancient fortifications once stood here, but they were destroyed by Louis XIII in 1622 owing to the pertinacious adhesion of the inhabitants to Calvinism. Pons is a charming town, and in the neighbourhood are two superb Romanesque churches, at Echebonne and Chadenac. That in the former has an arcaded north façade of noble proportions, while the church at Chadenac has an imposing triple portal surmounted by strange monsters.

Saintes, the capital of the ancient province of Saintonge, is a delightful and interesting town, somewhat neglected by the average guidebook. It was a flourishing centre of trade when Julius Cæsar conquered Gaul, and its important position under the Roman domination is shown by the great crumbling amphitheatre, which was built in the first century A.D., and also by the beautiful double arch erected in honour of the Emperor Tiberius. Saintes possesses two churches of outstanding merit: St. Eutope and the Abbaye des Dames de Notre Dame. The former has a superb Romanesque choir of the eleventh century, which now forms the nave, since the original was burnt by the Protestants in 1568. Below is a crypt of the same period which, with the exception of that at Chartres, is the largest in France. It would be difficult to exaggerate the beautiful proportions of this vast subterranean building, which for centuries lay buried and forgotten until it was unearthed and restored in 1842. This crypt has also the distinction of containing the tomb of the fourth-century St. Eutope, the first Bishop of Nantes, and of having received lyrical praise from Viollet-le-Duc, who was fortunately not concerned in its restoration.

The Abbaye des Dames de Notre Dame is a no less striking erection of the same period, crowned with a robust late eleventh-century tower. The simple recessed entrance leads into the interior with that fitness and assurance which gothic doorways, in their preoccupation with ornament, so often lack. The interior, with its single nave, seems to be in a chronic state of restoration. The abbey is situated, rather incongruously, in the barrack-square of a Senegalese garrison.

The road from Saintes to Cognac provides some of the most pleasing and typical scenery of France. Naturally in this district vineyards predominate, but they are broken by small woods with high timber and arable land lying in the valley by the river Charente. The straight, undulating roads are shadowed by limes and plane-trees. Cognac is historically important as the birthplace of François Ier, but some may regard it with greater respect as being the chief centre of the brandy trade of the world. Indeed, these apparently disconnected interests unite in the Château de Valois, where in 1494 the king was born, and which is now used by Monsieur Otard-Dupuy as his *chais*, or brandy warehouse. It is a pleasant experience to walk round the dark and spacious rooms of the château, speculating on the contents of the great barrels of Cognac standing by the bare walls which once were hung with Gobelin tapestries. Nearby, on the banks of the river, are two large *chais* with names familiar to English ears: those of Messrs. Martell and Hennessey.

The road between Cognac and Angoulême is flat, but the expanse of vineyards increases. The grapes which produce the *grande* or "Fine Champagne" are soon left behind for those of the "Petite Champagne," and, after Jarnac, the place of the latter are taken by the more general varieties responsible for the "Fins Bois." Although this road is devoid of scenic grandeur, those who enjoy a glass of good brandy will view these rich vineyards with pleasurable anticipation.

Angoulême, which is built on a hill between the valleys of the Charente and the Anguienne, is chiefly remarkable for its unusual Romanesque cathedral and the rampart boulevard surrounding the city, which affords, as may be anticipated, the most imposing views. The early twelfth-century cathedral is a curious Byzantine-Romanesque building which, although it has suffered sadly at the hands of seventeenth and nineteenth-century restorers, possesses a western façade as fine as any of its period in France. The intricate sculpture of the Last Judgment and the bold groups of St. George and the Dragon and St. Martin dividing his cloak with the beggar are conspicuous for their beauty of design. The exterior is further enhanced by the great cupola, rising above the cross of the transepts, and the high, flat tower, with its wealth of round arches, reminiscent of a Tuscan campanile. The interior of the cathedral contains nothing of interest but its out-line, and appears to be an entirely newly built church. This was the work of the late Monsieur Abadie, who seventy years ago planed all the walls and pillars down to a smooth, uniform surface, and filled the interstices of the stones with black mortar. The effect is too hideous to be described, and for this alone Monsieur Abadie takes his place in

102 A Waterway in Guyenne

3 A Cottage in the
Landes

104 Flooded Flats
the Vendée

105 A Reed-cutter of
Poitou

architectural history as one of the most vandalistic restorers of the nineteenth century.

The country in the modern department of Haute-Vienne, which is contiguous to Charente, is steeper and more thickly wooded than its neighbour, and across its deep valleys the small and variegated expanses of arable land look, in their different textures, like a patchwork quilt. This is the old province of Limousin, famous for its beef and cherry tarts, its *pâtés, cèpes*, and *lièvre à la royale*, and of course for its enamels. Limoges, the capital, consists of a large and undistinguished modern town built round the old city, which is dominated by the great tower of the Cathedral of St. Etienne. This tower, which stands alone and rests on the porch of the Romanesque church which existed before the present cathedral, was begun in 1273. It is a finely proportioned erection, and for a hundred years after its construction in 1242 served as a model for all Limousin architects. It is built in the gothic style of northern France, and comes as an unwelcome change after the pure Romanesque churches of Angoumois and Saintonge. The choir, however, is a good example of the period, and a beautiful vista can be enjoyed down the south aisle, with its fine groined roof and elegant groups of clustered columns. The tomb of Bishop Brun is also worth inspection for its statuettes and bas-reliefs, which include a vivid representation of Ste. Valerie presenting her head to St. Martial—a becoming present for the first Bishop of Limoges.

Near the cathedral lies the bishop's palace, a really delightful late eighteenth-century building. The ground floor contains some period furniture, but the remainder of the house is dedicated to a dreary mass exhibition of the products of Limoges. The terraced gardens which follow the line of the hills enjoy a lovely view, and readers of Balzac will recollect how in *Le Curé du Village* the Bishop took his dessert there, "in an arbour of vines at the angle of the lowest terrace," and in the company of three obsequious abbés discussed the affairs of Limoges. To-day all the episcopal terraces form part of the public gardens, and the ribbon growth of the city has sadly impaired the view.

Limoges has had a chequered history. The original town originated in the Roman period as a refuge from barbarian invasion. In the twelfth century Limousin came under English rule through that desirable heiress Eleanor of Aquitaine, but the inhabitants disliked the foreign domination and rebelled against it in 1370. The revolt failed, and the Black Prince taught the city a lesson by massacring three thousand men, women, and children. More pleasant is the reflection that as early as the seventh century Limoges was a centre of the goldsmith's art and of the minting of coins. The former industry had the rare distinction of being founded by a saint, and to-day St. Eloi is still the patron of the goldsmiths.   The manufacture of the world-famous Limoges enamels reached its zenith in craftsmanship, if not in taste, during the sixteenth century, and did not decay until two hundred years after.   Fortunately for the prosperity of the city the manufacture of porcelain then took the place of that of enamels, owing to the discovery of china clay at St. Yrieix in 1755.   Unfortunately for the reputation of Limoges enamel, however, that industry was revived in 1875. Limoges has three further claims to fame: President Sadi Carnot, apparently an inveterate "boulevardier" from the number of avenues called after him, was born there in 1837; the town gave its distinguished name to the limousine motor car; and, during the war, the expression *limogé* was given to lucky generals who had secured appointments at the base.

South-west of Limoges lies the road to the Dordogne, of which Perigueux, in the ancient province of Perigord, is the capital.   The Cathedral of St. Front in that city is one of the most curious churches in France, and, with its massive domes, presents a strangely Eastern appearance.   For some obscure reason the exact date of this building is unknown, but it is generally supposed to have been completed by the middle of the twelfth century.   It is constructed on the plan of a Greek cross, similar to that of St. Mark's at Venice, after which it is said to have been copied, with five superb domes—one over the crossing and one over each transept.   The tower, which is nearly two hundred feet high, consists of two cubes surmounted by a conical cupola with a delicate network pattern.   The exterior of the cathedral is otherwise mainly gothic, and it is supposed that in the architecture of St. Front that style made its first appearance in France.   The interior has been practically ruined by the hands of mid-nineteenth-century restorers, and once again, as at Angoulême, Monsieur Abadie is the chief villain in the tragedy.

Apart from St. Front, Perigueux is renowned as a gastronomic centre. Truffles grow in profusion in the neighbourhood, and its *pâtés*, particularly that of *Foie gras de Perdrix*, are famous.   Game abounds, and salmon and trout populate in great numbers the rivers of Dordogne, Isle, and Vezère.   Except for the Sauternes grapes of Brantôme, where on an island in the Dronne lived the Abbé de Brantôme, the great chronicler of sixteenth-century court life, Perigord is not rich in vineyards, although it produces a not unnaturally potent liqueur in *Eau-de-Vie de Prunes*.

West of Perigueux lies Riberac, possessing in its name the very common ending in the Dordogne of "ac," which is of course short for *aqua.* It is a sleepy little place on the Dronne, typical in its simple Romanesque church and pretty surroundings of many small towns in Perigord. Nearby lies Aubterre, with its ruined château ona precipitous limestone hill above the Dronne. Below, hewn out of the rock, is the empty and monolithic Church of St. Jean, probably worked in the eleventh century. The interior consists of an apse, a nave separated from a single aisle by great columns, and an immense vestibule probably of later date. The great height of the walls and the paucity of light impart to this gaunt and deserted church a forlorn and eerie atmosphere, which is substantially increased by the bones of Benedictine monks which are liberally strewn over the rocky floor.

On a plateau north of Aubterre lies the fascinating village of Chillac, with its simple Romanesque church of the twelfth century overshadowed by an elm-tree three hundred years old. Grouping prettily with the church rises the mediæval château, with its red roof and elegant *tourelles.* Chillac is actually in the department of the Charente, but from the neighbourhood of the château a superb view can be enjoyed over the Dordogne. It is indeed a most variegated and beautiful countryside. Tall woods are broken by fields of pasture and arable land, irrigated by the broad rivers which bring fertility to this happy region. Walnuts are also a speciality of the Dordogne, and the isolated tree of that genus, planted apparently at random, is a typical and delightful feature of the landscape. Vineyards, too, are not absent, and in the autumn many apple-trees, heavy with bright-red fruit, rise above the blue-green vines.

East of Perigueux lies perhaps the finest château in the Dordogne, that of Hautefort, which is situated on an abrupt hill between the rivers Lourde and Bauze. Built in the eleventh century, Hautefort was reconstructed about five hundred years later, but it retains all the grandeur and solidity of its earlier period. In the early thirteenth century Hautefort enjoyed the distinction of belonging to Bertrand de Born, who for a time was the favourite troubadour of Richard Cœur-de-Lion.

In the south-east portion of the Dordogne lies the picturesque town of Sarlat on the Cuze. Although the Church of St. Cyprien has a fine and massive Romanesque interior, Sarlat is chiefly notable for its beautiful old houses dating from the fourteenth to the sixteenth centuries. Perhaps the most remarkable of these is the François 1er home of Etienne de la Boëtie, Montaigne's beloved friend, who in his hatred of tyranny wrote his famous discourse on *Voluntary Servitude.* Bergerac, to the west of Sarlat, is not as pretty as its name; indeed, it is rare in the Dordogne to find a town of considerable importance with so little to recommend it.   Even the great duellist Cyrano de Bergerac, the hero of Rostand's romantic play, lived and died in Paris.

Just after leaving the Dordogne lies St. Emilion in the Gironde, the most picturesque and unspoilt town in the department.   The small hill on which it is situated is covered with a variety of beautiful buildings, many of which are half-caverned out of the rocks, similar to those at Les Baux in Provence.   The most important monument is the twelfth-century collegiate church, with its two stone Byzantine cupolas and the great gothic cloister built a hundred years later, in which each gallery has fourteen arches resting on two single columns.   Nearby rises the Château du Roi, built by Louis VIII in 1225, which is almost the sole Romanesque fortress in the Gironde.   Below it lies the monolithic church dedicated to St. Emilion, carved out of the rock by that saint and his companions during the eighth century.   The severe exterior is enlivened by a gothic portal, and the damp green rock-surfaces which form the interior are similar in height and appearance to those at Aubterre.   It is interesting to speculate on the reactions of this ascetic saint, who inhabited a dank cell nearby, to the strange coincidence that, while he passes almost unmentioned in the Roman Calendar, the name of the red wine called after him enjoys a hedonistic and international reputation.

The chief town of the Gironde and the capital of the ancient province of Guyenne is Bordeaux on the Garonne.   This is the fourth largest town in France and the third most important port after Le Havre and Marseilles; but in the opinion of the visitor it will have the even greater distinction of possessing as beautiful civic buildings and general lay-out as any town in the country, with the obvious exception of Paris. Bordeaux has been a prosperous city since the days of the Romans, when it flourished under the gay name of Burdigala.   From the middle of the twelfth century and for the subsequent three hundred years it was held by the English, and the Black Prince, when not engaged in sacking towns in France or "building castles in Spain," held his court there.   His son, later Richard II, was in fact born at Bordeaux.   The defeat of Talbot, however, at the Battle of Castillon in 1453 restored the city permanently to the French crown, although the inhabitants joined the Fronde insurrection in the seventeenth century when Bordeaux successfully withstood a memorable siege by the troops of Louis XIV.   A hundred years later commercial prosperity caused the erection of most of the fine buildings in the city, and the restraint of its people during the Revolution enabled them to form the moderate, but short-lived, Girondist party.   Among many well-known Bordelais are numbered Ausonius, the fourth-century Latin poet, that desirable heiress Eleanor of

Aquitaine, and two popular painters, Carle Vernet and Rosa Bonheur.

The brilliant eighteenth-century planning makes it comparatively easy for the stranger to acquire a general idea of the central portion of Bordeaux, and the most important ecclesiastical and civic buildings fall naturally into three main divisions.   The first and principal division consists of a triangle, comprising the chief commercial centre, and formed by the Cours de l'Intendance, the Cours Georges Clemenceau, and the Allées de Tourny.   At the three angles of this rough triangle lie the Place Gambetta, the Place de la Comédie, and the Place Tourny. In the middle of the triangle is situated the Place des Grands Hommes, now used as a fish-market.   Each of the three former squares is outstanding either for its lay-out or the individual buildings which embellish it.

The Place Gambetta is a beautiful Louis XV composition, while in the Place de la Comédie stands the superb theatre built between 1773 and 1780 by Victor Louis, who was also responsible for the galleries of the Palais Royal in Paris.   The great classical colonnade on the entrance front, consisting of twelve Corinthian columns supporting a high balcony crowned with statues of the Muses and Graces, imparts an almost unique beauty amongst theatres to Louis's creation.   The interior, above the vestibule, contains a concert hall of noble proportions with a ceiling painted by Bouguereau, and the wide expanse of the grand staircase, which is suitably ornamented with a statue of Victor Louis himself, leads to the circular auditorium where the National Assembly held its session in 1871.   It will be recollected that Bordeaux was the seat of the French Government both at that date and again in 1914.

The Place Tourny is named after Aubert de Tourny, who in the second half of the eighteenth century was chiefly responsible for the spectacular lay-out of Bordeaux.   The symmetry of this square has unfortunately been spoilt, but its original elevation can be judged by the delightful Hôtel de la Marine and the two adjacent corner houses. The Place Tourny leads to the spacious Place des Quinconces on the Quai Louis XVIII.   In the middle of this public garden lies the Monument des Girondins, a splendid example of a fountain in the "Art Nouveau" manner.   In this vigorous, if chaotic, composition, statues representing Bordeaux, the Dordogne, the Garonne, Eloquence, and History, assisted by four rampant seahorses, struggle in the wildest confusion round a semi-nude figure of Liberty.

The second principal artistic division of the city is that of the Place de la Bourse and its neighbourhood, lying on the north bank of the

15

Garonne. This square, which has the most beautiful architectural design of any in Bordeaux, was built by Jacques Gabriel between 1738 and 1755. The Bourse itself, which was finished in 1749, is balanced on the left by the Douane, erected ten years earlier. The three streets which radiate from the square are planned with the skill of theatrical perspective. Nearby are two monuments of fifteenth-century architecture; the Church of St. Pierre and the delightful Port de Caillau, a machicolated gothic gateway with pointed roofs of different elevations.

The third division into which Bordeaux has been arbitrarily divided in these pages contains the cathedral and the Hôtel de Ville. Despite the considerable beauty of the east front, with its elegant buttresses of the fifteenth century, the Cathedral of St. André cannot be regarded as a highly successful work. The great aisleless nave of the twelfth century seems to lack inspiration and to be disconnected from the lofty choir, which is itself a fine example of the *rayonnant* gothic style. The sinister figure of Monsieur Abadie, however, once more emerges, not only as the restorer of the interior, but also as the destroyer of the cloister which had previously existed by the south transept. Detached from the cathedral rises the late fifteenth-century Tour Pey-Berland, much disfigured by the vast gold statue of Our Lady of Aquitaine perched on the spire.

The Hôtel de Ville, standing by the western front of the cathedral, is a fine classical building erected by Etienne for Archbishop Rohan between 1770 and 1780. It is approached through a beautiful screen ornamented with Doric columns and high ironwork grilles with round arches. An extensive museum of painting and sculpture occupies the principal rooms of the Hôtel de Ville, which, besides having housed archbishops and mayors, was used as a royal palace by Napoleon in 1808, and again by Louis XVIII in 1816.

Two other buildings in Bordeaux merit a visit : the churches of Ste. Croix and Notre Dame. The eleventh-century façade of the former is singularly lacking in proportion, and it is not surprising to learn that it was restored by Monsieur Abadie. The bleak interior, however, possesses some of the finest Romanesque capitals in France. But more typical of the urbane spirit of Bordeaux, which is so infectious to any visitor of sensibility, is the Church of Notre Dame. Although an attempt has been made to give the exterior the impression of a church, it has been practically abandoned in the interior which, with its gilded *boiseries*, marbled pilasters, and wealth of amorini, has the appearance of a magnificent ballroom in some royal home.

To the north of Bordeaux lie the extensive vineyards which produce

Medoc, a wine so delicious in the country of its origin, but with a name which in England imparts a certain feeling of melancholy owing to its cheap position in the average wine-list.   A journey south-east in the direction of Agen will take the traveller first through the Graves and then through the smaller Sauternes vineyards.   In the latter the grapes of Château Yquem are, of course, world-famous.   The small town of Barsac is nearby, with a delightful eighteenth-century church surrounded by the sweet grapes of its vineyard.   To the west of this great tract of grape-producing country stretch the long and narrow salt plains which, with Arcachon as their principal town, are renowned for the delicious *mouton de pré salé*.

After Langon, south-east of Bordeaux, the vineyards terminate and the department of Lot-et-Garonne, originally included in Guyenne, is reached.   Agen, the capital, is an old town with narrow streets crossed by modern boulevards.   The Cathedral of St. Caprais has an imposing twelfth-century apse, with transepts of the same period, but the interior is spoilt by the hideous late nineteenth-century paintings which cover the wall surfaces.   Agen is famous for the elegant shapes of the Agenais cattle and for its stuffed plums, which are eagerly consumed in all parts of the world.

The modern department of Tarn-et-Garonne lies on the border of the ancient provinces of Guyenne and Languedoc, and has as its chief town Montauban on the Tarn.   It is rather smoky and ill-planned, although many attractive red-brick houses of the fifteenth and sixteenth centuries show the wide influence of the architecture of Toulouse.   In particular, the Church of St. Jacques, built at the beginning of the fifteenth century in the Tolosan gothic style, is remarkable for its magnificent octagonal tower.   The Cathedral of Notre Dame makes a charming contrast to St. Jacques.   It was completed in 1739 by the architect Larroque in a severe classical style.   The interior, which is planned as a Greek cross, is chiefly notable for the "Vow of Louis XIII," by Jean-Dominique Ingres, which ornaments the sacristy.   This great artist was a native of Montauban, and showed his appreciation of his native town by bequeathing it a superb collection of his own drawings.

The department of Gers, which lies south-west of Tarn-et-Garonne, was originally in the northern half of Gascony.   Auch, the capital, possesses a cathedral in which are over a hundred oak stalls, all masterpieces of the early Renaissance period.   Auch, however, is more noted as an important gastronomic centre.   Besides Armagnac and sparkling wines, the "Côtes du Gers," geese and ducks are bred in great quantities in the neighbourhood, producing a *foie gras* to rival that of

Strasbourg.   Two dishes for which Gers is famous are *cèpes au vin blanc* and *civet de lièvre à l'Armagnac*.   This part of Gascony is as broken by rivers as any province in France.   Of these the most important, from east to west, are the Garonne, the Gers, the Baise, the Osse, the Arros, and the Adour.

West of the department of Gers lies that of the Landes, which, stretching down the Atlantic coast, formed the most westerly portion of Gascony.   This district is the most barren in France, and in the eighteenth century it appeared as if the wind-blown sand would turn it into an uninhabitable desert.   The engineer Nicolas Brémontier, however, successfully checked this destructive inroad by planting the great pine-forests which are now the distinctive feature of the Landes. Many of these woods are of great beauty, and it is interesting to see the extensive timber-yards and the picturesque rustic cottages which nestle under the trees.   Apart from the forests, the department is famous for the *courses landaises*, a bloodless and rather ridiculous variety of the Spanish bull-fight.   It is, however, entertaining to watch the antics of the mature and long-suffering *vaches de combat* which pursue the clumsy *toreros*, and usually a number of participating spectators, with such craft and complacency.

Mont-de-Marsan, the chief town in the Landes, is prettily situated on the banks of the Douze and the Midou, but although it is the centre of a wide country district, the lack of any buildings of distinction or antiquity show the great poverty of the Landes in the past centuries. Dax, to the south, is well known for its mud-baths and hot springs, but it is a most uninteresting place, and St. Sever to the east is the only town in the department which can boast of a building of real importance. This is the church, dedicated to its martyred patron, which was erected during the tenth and twelfth centuries.   The choir, with its seven apsides with cradle or ribbed vaulting, is exceptionally beautiful, as are also the great marble Roman columns which, in the early Romanesque period, were adorned with their present capitals, boldly carved with massive foliage and fantastic beasts.

The Biscay seaboard of the Landes is remarkably deserted, and it is not until after Bayonne is reached, just in the department of the Basses-Pyrénées, that the barren coast becomes the thickly populated area of which Biarritz is the famous centre.   Biarritz is considerably the largest resort on the Bay of Biscay, and its fine strand, merging into a rocky coast of small bays, destined it for eventual popularity.   Victor Hugo, indeed, foreshadowed this development when he visited Biarritz during the reign of King Louis-Philippe.   "Nowhere else have I seen old Neptune destroying Cybele with more power, joyousness, or grace.

On all this coast there is abundance of noise," wrote the poet; and he was right, since the white foam which breaks over the Rocher de la Vierge and the Côte de Basques has given to the whole of this seaboard the name of the Côte d'Argent.   Then Monsieur Hugo continued: "I have only one misgiving—it may become fashionable."

Biarritz began to change from a little fishing-village to a great seaside resort in the year 1838, when, during the first Carlist war, Spanish exiles, no longer permitted to enjoy the amenities of San Sebastian, discovered its pleasant possibilities.   A few years later Eugénie de Montijo, the future Empress of the French, came there with her mother, although she was not, as many guidebooks assert, a Carlist refugee.   Her visit, however, was vital to the development of Biarritz, since, in 1855, after her marriage to Napoleon III, she erected on the northern promontory above the little town the Villa Eugénie, which became her favourite summer residence.   The villa was built of English bricks, a fact of which the Empress was perhaps unreasonably proud.   Eugéne Boudin has often depicted the gay imperial court being blown along the sandy seashore, the Empress leading in her short crinoline and button boots; and he has also painted it as a conversation piece, with the amorous Emperor in his top-hat and black frock-coat sitting amid a group of appreciative ladies.   Count Bismarck, who paid a visit to the Villa Eugénie in 1867, must have been an incongruous and perhaps inauspicious figure in this carefree and glamorous company.

After the fall of the Second Empire, Biarritz suffered a short eclipse, although the Empress's villa was shortly incorporated in the present Hôtel du Palais.   But the visit of Queen Victoria in 1889, followed by those of King Edward VII in nearly every year of his reign, made it the most fashionable resort on the Atlantic coast.   Indeed, the affection of the opulent English for their amiable monarch, who became such a familiar figure on the *plage* in his grey "Homburg" and Inverness cape, induced them to go there in February and March, probably the two coldest months in the year.   Biarritz is further connected with royalty by the happy incidence that at the Villa Mouriscot, then the home of the hospitable Princess Frederica of Hanover, King Alfonso XIII was betrothed to Princess Ena of Battenberg.

To-day Biarritz is as vulgar and overcrowded as any large seaside resort in France or England, but in the month of May, before the herds of holiday-makers litter the Grande Plage with their naked forms, it is still possible to visualise the Empress with her ladies emerging from her red-brick villa in pork-pie hat and crinoline, to take her morning exercise along this broad stretch of yellow sand.

CHAPTER VIII

THE PYRENEES

THE Pyrenees are generally considered to be a wall of mountains with a single watershed, running east and west from the Mediterranean to the Atlantic, and conveniently separating the French and Spanish peoples. Such a conception, however, is wide of the truth, since the Pyrenees are formed of two chains of mountains, one running north of west from the Mediterranean and the other south of east from the Atlantic. Nor do these two chains meet, since there is a gap between them of eight miles south of St. Gaudens. Again, the Pyrenees do not divide ethnologically the inhabitants of France and Spain. On the contrary, they cut across them in the most arbitrary manner, leaving both Basques and Catalans on either side of the political frontiers. These two races occupy together at the western and eastern extremities of the Pyrenees about half their total length, while in the centre of the chain lie the ancient territorial divisions of Béarn, Bigorre, Comminge, and Foix, which in the fifteenth century formed the northern portion of the Kingdom of Navarre.

These three racial divisions are clearly emphasised by the physical nature of the Pyrenees. The Basque race occupies the valleys from the Atlantic coastline to the Pic d'Anie, south of Oloron, where it abruptly terminates, while the Catalans, spreading westwards from the Mediterranean, reach as far as the Carlitte mountains, which tower over the frontier town of Bourg-Madame. Between them lies Navarre. It may be convenient to consider the different peoples and the countries they inhabit travelling eastwards from the Atlantic to the Mediterranean.

"What are the Basques?" M. Voltaire once enquired—and himself answered the question with some asperity: "Why, a little people which dances at the foot of the Pyrenees!" Something more of this ancient and strange race is fortunately known, although the Roman historians ignored this virile remnant of the Iberian people, despite the incidence that a great imperial road passed through Basque territory. But in the remote past the Basques inhabited all Aquitaine from the Loire, western Spain, and northern Portugal. To-day, when they are restricted to a few provinces on either side of the Western Pyrenees, they still maintain a sturdy independence towards their respective governments and a great attachment for their obscure and complicated mother-tongue, which, tradition asserts, the Devil himself was unable to master even after a seven years' sojourn amongst them.

The inner councils of the Basques are run by a matriarchy which the men appear to have accepted since the remote past. The outward indication of this unyielding form of government can be seen on Sundays after Mass, when groups of severe matrons, all robed in black, assemble outside their houses to settle questions of local significance. From these important conferences the male is rigidly excluded—and naturally there is no suffragette movement amongst the Basques. The ladies are already too powerful to need the vote.

Pelota and the beret are peculiarly associated with the Basques in the popular mind, and it is interesting to recollect that while the French Basques wear the tight-fitting beret, their brothers in Spain adopt a larger and more amorphous variety of this becoming cap. Another custom—now, alas! nearly extinct amongst the Basques—is that of the *Couvade*. In past times a woman immediately after childbirth would leave her bed in order to resume her normal household duties, and her place would be taken by the husband, who, with the baby in his arms, would receive the congratulations of the relatives and be fed on pap and broth for ten days. This astonishing custom is said to have been founded on the belief that woman was merely a machine for the production of children, who belonged, body and soul, to the man. In any case, the practice is now probably dead, and Basque fathers can no longer look forward to the ascetic leisure connected with ten days' assumption of spurious motherhood.

Bayonne, on the Adour, is the capital of the Basque country, but it is a town of charm rather than of importance. The ramparts, built by Vauban and now laid out as a promenade, are perhaps its most pleasant feature, and although the much restored gothic cathedral is a rather dreary structure, the arms of the House of Plantagenet and of the Talbot family, amongst others, are an interesting reminder that for three hundred years during the Middle Ages Bayonne belonged to the English crown. The town prospered under this foreign rule owing to a flourishing wine trade with England and Ireland, and the people of Bayonne offered a stiff resistance to Dunois, Charles VII's general, who eventually reduced it in 1451. Bayonne has also the merit of being the birthplace of Léon Bonnat, whose collection of drawings, which he bequeathed to the nation, is one of the finest in France. As its name implies, the town has also the less amiable distinction of having been responsible, in the seventeenth century, for the invention of the pugnacious bayonet.

The so-called "Pays de Labourd," in which Bayonne is situated, is one of the most fertile districts of the Pyrenees. The Western Pyrenees, it must be remembered, differ profoundly from the eastern chain of the same mountains in that they intercept and condense the vapours from the Atlantic, and their lower slopes are therefore profusely clothed with such deciduous trees as birch, walnut, and chestnut, while the conifers above them give way on the summit of the mountains to heather and scrub. The Eastern Pyrenees, lacking similar rains, are white and barren, and the heavy glaciers of the west are there unknown.

The valley of the Labourd is typical of the Western Pyrenees, with its varied cultivation and frequent villages, separated by fine stretches of timber which give the landscape a pleasant air of domesticity. To the east, the valley of the Soule has a similar prosperous appearance, and has for its capital Mauléon, lying on the banks of the Saison. This picturesque little town, dominated by the ruins of a fifteenth-century château, lay dead for many years until recently the manufacture of "espadrilles" has restored it to prosperity. Nearby, in the same luxuriant valley of the Saison, lie two villages of some interest to the student of nineteenth-century French literature: Troisville, from which Dumas took the name of Tréville in his *Three Musketeers*, and Aramits, after which he called the tallest and leanest of his heroes.

Below the valley of the Soule, on the Spanish frontier, lies Basse-Navarre, the capital of which is St. Jean-Pied-de-Port, so called from its position at the entrance to the pass of Roncesvalles, which connects upper and lower Navarre. This is a fascinating town, with two lines of ramparts and a lofty citadel restored by Vauban in the seventeenth century. The precipitous street leading to this citadel contains some beautiful houses of the sixteenth and seventeenth centuries, many of which are built of red sandstone and are obligingly inscribed with the dates of erection over their front doors. St. Jean is also renowned for its crayfish, which, to satisfy the taste of a gourmet, should be cooked in white wine and burnt brandy.

South of St. Jean lies the famous pass of Roncesvalles, which, besides enabling the Duke of Wellington to continue his pursuit of Marshal Soult into France, is celebrated in the *Song of Roland* as the place where the Paladin Roland and the twelve peers of the Emperor Charlemagne were crushed to death by rocks flung on to their heads by the treacherous Basques. This method of attack cheated Roland of the advantage he had previously enjoyed with his mighty sword "Durandal." This sword, which further east in the Pyrenees, below Gavarnie, was responsible, in legend, for the great fissure in the rocks called the "Brèche de Roland," was ornamented with a pommel of heavy gold, reputed to contain a tooth of St. Peter, a few drops of the blood of St. Basil, and a lock of St. Denis's hair.

Due north of Basse-Navarre and Soule lies Orthez, the ancient capital of Béarn and a town of considerable importance in the history of France. Béarn had been an independent viscounty until the close of the thirteenth century, when an heiress married the Count of Foix, a contiguous ruler, and thereby united the two countries. Their great-grandson, Gaston Phœbus X, who was born in 1331, was one of the most picturesque sovereigns of mediæval France. On account of his beauty he was given the name of Phœbus, and he adopted as his crest a blazing sun. Opulent, lascivious, and a patron of the arts, Gaston was visited by Froissart when the latter was writing the history of Gascony. Of him Froissart wrote: "Gaston Phœbus was a prudent knight, full of enterprise and wisdom. He never allowed men of abandoned character to be about his person; he . . . was constant at his devotions." Nevertheless, Gaston murdered his brother and his only son, together with fifteen of the latter's companions, on the false charge of attempting to murder him. "Which was a pity," wrote Froissart, "for there were not in all Gascony such handsome and well-appointed squires."

Gaston Phœbus's death was fitting for such a glamorous and hasty ruler. He died suddenly from the contact of cold water with which he was washing the blood off his hands after a bear hunt at Sauveterre de Béarn. But it was probably the death Gaston would have chosen, since in his book, the *Miroyr des Deduicts de la Chasse*, he wrote with astonishing optimism: "We escape the Seven Mortal Sins . . . for good hunters will in this world have joys, sports, diversions, and after-wards Paradise."

Sauveterre, the scene of Gaston's death, is perhaps the most pic-turesque little town in Béarn. Above the Gave d'Oloron stand the plain façade of the Romanesque church, the lofty Tour Montréal, and the ancient ramparts of the town. Below, by the wide and swiftly flowing river, lies the mediæval manor-house, now converted into an excellent hotel, where Gaston Phœbus probably died. Nearby, the decaying structure of an ivy-clad bridge fails to stretch across the Gave and ends abruptly in a crumbling tower. The steep slope between the manor-house and the town is clothed with a luxuriant and most variegated vegetation. Willows, acacias, and magnolias mingle freely with almond and banana-trees.

After the death of Gaston Phœbus X, Orthez declined in fame until the sixteenth century, when an heiress, Catherine of Foix and Béarn, married Jean d'Albret of Navarre, thus uniting the three countries

16

under the latter crown.   Their granddaughter, Jeanne d'Albret, who was also an heiress, was destined by her vigorous adhesion to Calvinism to bring an unenviable renown to the quiet town of Orthez.   On the death of her husband, Antoine de Bourbon, in 1562, Jeanne publicly embraced Protestantism, and although she was compelled as a result to seek refuge in La Rochelle, she commissioned a certain Count Montgomery to convert her dominions by force to Calvinism.   This fiery Scot took Orthez in the summer of the same year and, not content with murdering all the lay inhabitants, compelled the Carmelites to jump into their own well until they had choked it up, while the "Cordeliers" friars, whose monastery stood high above the river, were pushed from their windows into the waters below.   This massacre took place on August 24th—the Feast of St. Bartholomew.

To-day moribund, Orthez contains few monuments dating from those violent times except the "Vieux Bourg," with its mediæval houses, and the superb remains of the fourteenth-century "Pont Vieux," defended on the central span by its elegant watch-tower.   Nearby are the sharp rocks in the Gave below the monastery of the "Cordeliers" friars.

Nine years before Jeanne plunged her patrimony into the blood-bath of Calvinism, she had been summoned by her father, Henri II of Navarre, to Pau, as she was about to be confined.   Jeanne obeyed, and on December 13th, 1553, gave birth to a boy destined to become Henri IV, King of France as well as of Navarre.   Legend relates that during her parturition Jeanne had the courage to sing a pious song to please her father, and that the latter, after rubbing the child's lips with garlic, poured into his mouth a few drops of the delicious local wine from Jurançon, in order to ensure that his eventual heir should be a true Béarnais.

Pau is naturally very proud of Henri IV, and a statue of the king gazes from the shade of the Place Royale towards the Boulevard des Pyrénées: a land view which, according to Lamartine, was like the sea view at Naples—the finest in the world.   But in that distinguished author's day no roaring railway junction made a disturbing foreground along the Gave of the Pau.   Further along the terrace from the Place Royale the château raises its ugly façade, which is only relieved by the magnificent red-brick *donjon* built by Gaston Phœbus in the fourteenth century.   The interior of the château, although entirely dismantled, is hung with many superb Gobelin and Flemish tapestries.   The second floor, which contains an exquisite needlework bed of the time of Louis XIV, was for some time occupied by Abd-el-Kader, King Louis-Philippe's distinguished Algerian prisoner; but the Emir and his

106 The Foothills of the Pyrenees

107 Pau: Boulevard des Pyrénées

108   A Hilltop Church in the Pyrenees: St. Bertrand-de-Comminges

109   A Crag Castle in the Pyrenees: Tours de Foix

wives had such dirty habits that, in 1848, they were removed to more austere apartments at the château of Amboise.

Of more historical interest is Henri IV's cradle, in the room in which he is said to have been born. This cradle is made from a single tortoise-shell suspended above a table covered with blue velvet embroidered with lilies and the king's monogram. It is surmounted by a plumed helmet and an array of silk flags. It is now officially denied that the original cradle was destroyed at the time of the Revolution and that the present one dates from the First Empire. In appearance, however, this delightful erection has none of the robustness of Jeanne d'Albret's period and much of the sophisticated manner of the early nineteenth century.

A distinguished but later fellow-citizen of Pau than Henri IV was Charles Bernadotte, who was born there in 1764. They had, however, one characteristic in common: they both abjured the religions of their birth in order to obtain a throne. As is well known Henri IV, born a Calvinist, considered Paris to be worth a Mass, while Bernadotte, a Catholic by birth, became a Lutheran in order to obtain the crown of Sweden.

But it is not to Jeanne d'Albret, Henri IV, or to Bernadotte that Pau owes its prominence to-day, but rather to the incidence that, in the year 1816, after many winters spent by force of circumstances in their own country, the English discovered that Pau was blessed with a mild and healthy climate. From then onwards the influx of visitors increased, reaching its height during the early years of the present century. But to-day, despite the amenity of hunting in the neighbour-hood, Pau is but a shadow of its former self, and through the deserted halls of its great hotels and along the wide stretches of its once fashion-able promenades the visitor will feel the passage of dim Edwardian ghosts. Nevertheless, and perhaps owing to this graceful decay, many should enjoy a winter at Pau, in particular the resident of Bloomsbury, since the *Guide Bleu* assures its readers that the climate is particularly suitable to "overworked intellectuals."

On a clear day the view from the terrace at Pau will embrace the twin peaks of the Midi and the Ossau, the latter of which lies at the end of the valley of that name, close to the Spanish frontier. Just west of the valley of the Ossau lies the valley of the Aspe, and these two valleys form the platform for the great Roman road which runs from the French plains through the pass of Somport and on to Saragossa. The opening of the valley of the Aspe lies just south of Oloron and Oloron-Ste.-Marie, two contiguous towns situated above the Gave of the Aspe and that of the Ossau. Both towns possess a cathedral, Ste. Croix at

Oloron, built in the eleventh century, being crowned with a remarkable Byzantine dome and containing aisle-vaults in the Auvergne style.   At Oloron-Ste.-Marie the cathedral has a massive square tower of the twelfth century and a choir of the fourteenth, which is a masterpiece of the delicate *rayonnant* manner.

The valley of the Aspe is as fascinating as any in the Pyrenees.   It forms a clean-cut gorge with high, barren hills on either side, while down in the plain fields of maize and sweet-corn are broken by vine-yards and small woods of oaks and chestnuts.   Tall plane-trees line the roads of this remote and silent valley.   The valley of the Ossau, which is less cultivated, is densely clothed with forests and shut in by bleak and towering mountains.   It is said to have inspired Gustave Doré with the ideas for some of the more sinister of his pictorial backgrounds.

At the end of this valley lie the thermal springs at Eaux-Chaudes, a straggling town which, from the proximity of the mountains and con-sequent lack of sun, is not very tempting as a health resort.   High above this sad town and at the foot of the Pic du Midi d'Ossau is situated the little hamlet of Gabas, which is said to be one of the last remaining haunts of the Pyrenean bear and the best locality for stalking the agile chamois.   These valleys are also noted for their wild flowers, which are considered by botanical experts to rival those of the Alps. Amongst many varieties, saxifrage, wild geranium, purple toothwort, blue monk's-hood, and the Alpine rose grow in profusion.   Both the valleys of the Aspe and the Ossau, owing to their fascinating inter-mixture of wildness and cultivation and the great bleak mountains that tower above their spacious plains, are as interesting and romantic as any in the Pyrenees.

Travelling east, rather than south, from Pau, Tarbes is reached, whence radiate three diverse valleys: those of Lourdes, Arreau, and Bigorre.   Tarbes itself, which is the ancient capital of Bigorre, is an ugly town situated on the Adour, with a graceless cathedral of brick, stone, and rolled pebbles.   It has, however, the distinction of being the birthplace of the Jacobin Bertrand Barrère, of whom Macaulay wrote: "In him the qualities which are the proper objects of hatred and the qualities which are the proper objects of contempt preserve an exquisite and absolute harmony."   In strange contrast to this blood-thirsty and long-lived revolutionary, Tarbes was also the birthplace of Théophile Gautier and Marshal Foch.

The most westerly of the valleys radiating from Tarbes, that of Lourdes, has on its western extremity the remarkable pilgrimage church of Notre Dame de Bétharram, situated in the town of that name, which is also famous for its stalactite caverns.   The original church, which was destroyed by the orders of Jeanne d'Albret, was rebuilt in 1614, and its exterior resembles a modest château of that period. The interior, however, is decorated in the most fanciful Spanish manner, with crude gilt ornamentation and a reredos which would be more in place in Andalusia than in southern France. The organ loft has the merit of being the pious offering of Napoleon III.

Following the valley along the Gave of the Pau, the first view of Lourdes, with its bright conglomeration of religious buildings and its austere and precipitously situated château, is unexpected and impressive. The château, in which is now housed a somewhat melancholy museum of Pyrenean exhibits, has the distinction of being the last stronghold in Guyenne retained by the English. It did not surrender until 1418, but only the fourteenth-century keep and the Tour de Garnabie, on the ramparts, bear witness to that historic occasion.

Since Lourdes is the most famous pilgrim resort of the Catholic world, those interested in mass psychology will enjoy a rare and perhaps stimulating experience from the animation in its streets and in the precincts of the miraculous Grotto. It is unfortunate, however, that although the Church of the Rosary and the Basilica above it are built in the most elaborate manner and of the most expensive materials, these edifices are mean in conception and hideous from the æsthetic point of view. It is indeed to be regretted that so much sincere religious fervour has not been given the opportunity to blossom against a more dignified and artistic background.

Further down the valley of Lourdes lies Cauterets Spa. Fashionable since the sixteenth century, when Marguerite de Valois, Queen of Navarre, composed there in her spare moments the obscene *Heptameron*, it has also been patronised by Queen Hortense, the mother of Napoleon III, as well as by his eventual wife, Eugénie de Montijo, who came there in the 'forties with her mother, after their temporary expulsion from the court of Queen Isabel II of Spain. Both bathing and gargling can be enjoyed at Cauterets in a variety of health-giving springs, but the chief attraction for invalids and convalescents has always been the Thermes des Œufs, so called from the sulphurated hydrogen emitted by these waters, which smell like rotten eggs.

The second valley leading southward from Tarbes is that of Bigorre, like Lourdes somewhat overcrowded in the summer, in which the chief town is Bagnères-de-Bigorre, picturesquely situated on the Adour at the foot of Mount Bédat. This health resort is so ancient and distinguished that it was even mentioned with approbation by Montaigne and visited by Laurence Sterne. It is certainly less vulgar than Eaux-Chaudes and Cauterets. A little further down the valley lies the sixteenth-century

village of Campan, which is famous for its marble.   Here was quarried
the marble for the peristyle of the Grand Trianon, for a score of
columns for the Royal Palace in Berlin, and for the interior decoration of
Garnier's *flamboyant* opera-house in Paris.

The third valley radiating from Tarbes, that of the Arreau, is the
longest enclosed valley in the Pyrenees.   Above its wide and cultivated
plain rise in the distance the great semicircles of precipices called
Cirques which, always distinctive of the Pyrenees, are a salient feature of
this region.   Arreau itself has a pleasant fifteenth-century castellated
church, and a few miles beyond lies the ruined castle of Bordères, which
was built in the twelfth century by the ferocious Counts of Armagnac,
who at that period owned a strip of territory from the Garonne to the
Pyrenees.

A short distance south-east of the valley of Arreau lies the southern
portion of the valley of Luchon, enshrining the fashionable spa of that
name, whose waters are mentioned as the most health-giving in the
Pyrenees as far back as the first century A.D.   The valley, however, is
more interesting than the town, since the former lies in the very centre
of the Pyrenean mountain system, where the eastern and western
chains divide.   It is also the last of the wide, flat valleys running north
and south, several of which have been cursorily described in these
pages.   After Luchon, great groups of barren hills tend to replace the
indented and more kindly valleys of the Western Pyrenees.

At the northern mouth of the valley of Luchon lies the decayed city
of St. Bertrand-de-Comminges, which, in the Cathedral of Notre
Dame, possesses the most beautiful and interesting church in the
Pyrenees.   The exterior is more remarkable for its general position,
crowning the summit of a small isolated hill against a background of
dark mountains, than for any outstanding architectural merits, although
the crowd of buttresses which support it on all sides seem to indicate
the existence of a very precious interior.   The church is entered
through a severe Romanesque narthex, but, after the first bay is passed,
the grey walls blossom into the sophisticated *rayonnant* style.   It is the
Renaissance choir, begun in 1537, however, which is the cathedral's
finest possession.   The rood loft, choir screen, and stalls are exquisitely
carved in bas-relief, and with a wealth of figures both sacred and profane.
Humour was clearly not deficient in the artists responsible, since one
group consisting of a pair of monkeys struggling for the possession of a
thick stick is obviously meant to portray two ecclesiastics fighting for
the office of abbot, while the two representations of a monk being
birched must have proved amusing distractions to the religious in choir.
On the south side of the cathedral the Romanesque cloister, miniature

110   A Village in the Pyrenees: Arrens

111   The Cloister of Elne

112, 113   Bullock Transport in the Pyrenees

in size and delicate in construction, enjoys a superb view over the valley of the Garonne.

St. Gaudens, to the north of Comminges, is an uninteresting town except for its restored Romanesque church and for the fact that it was the birthplace of the pugnacious St. Raymond, the founder of the Spanish military order of Calatrava in the twelfth century. The road, however, from Comminges to St. Girons is full of scenic incident and sufficiently precipitous to be reminiscent of a "mountain railway." Leaving the wide valley of the Garonne at Fronsac and joining the Route des Pyrénées, the road ascends to the well-timbered Col des Ares, with a beautiful view of the Pays de Comminge below. The low Col de Buret is then crossed before the steep and twisting ascent through the Ger valley to the Col du Portet d'Aspet, which is a particularly bleak and ill-favoured mountain. The road then descends sharply through a succession of dreary villages to the fertile valley of the Lez, at the end of which is situated St. Girons. Despite the great fluctuations in altitude, this road is remarkable for the similarity of the villages and vegetation through which it passes. Pleasing to the eye, however, are the wide and bright-green slopes ascending from the road, where the grass has been cut by hand, which bestow on the adjacent scenery an almost domestic atmosphere contrasting strangely with the great forest-clad mountains above.

St. Girons is an uninteresting town, but just above it lies the picturesque village of St. Lizier, with its fine Romanesque church, remarkable for the high brick fourteenth-century tower, typical of the Tolosan style of that period. The Romanesque cloisters are also beautiful and well preserved. Above the church rises the gay façade of the eighteenth-century bishop's palace. It is now used as a lunatic asylum, to which entrance may sometimes be obtained, although not without some natural difficulty. St. Girons, which since the thirteenth century had belonged to the county of Foix, passed with the latter into the Kingdom of Navarre two hundred years later.

Foix itself, which lies at the confluence of the Ariège and the Arget, is a sleepy and fascinating town dominated by an abrupt rock on which stand three isolated towers, the ruins of a once impregnable fortress. When the sun shines on the bleak mountain behind them, the "Tours de Foix" present from the St. Girons road a most stirring and romantic spectacle. The town below the rock contains one outstanding seventeenth-century house, the Maison des Cariatides, and the general disposition of the squares and streets gives it an air of comfort and prosperity.

The history of the town, however, has been far from happy, since in the twelfth century it became one of the chief centres of the Albigensian movement.   This heresy, which had originated with the earlier Manichees, who believed in the dualism of good and evil principles, made a great appeal to the people of southern France, who for a time seemed eager to relapse into their pagan past.   The heresy was condemned in 1176 by the Council of Albi, from which the Albigensians derived their name, but the Counts of Toulouse and Foix declined to interfere with the beliefs of a growing section of their subjects.   The subsequent crusade against the Albigensians, led by Simon de Montfort, devastated the rich and fertile country of Languedoc and was accompanied by the atrocities inevitable in any religious conflict.   When Count Roger Bernard of Foix at last submitted in 1240 to the superior forces of orthodoxy, his subjects had been decimated and his patrimony destroyed.

Count Raymond of Toulouse, who, together with the Count of Foix, had been a powerful supporter of his heretical subjects, governed a city which, politically and commercially, possessed a similar importance for the French inhabitants of the Pyrenees as did Saragossa for the Spaniards on the southern slopes of the mountains.   Toulouse to-day retains one outstanding example of its wealth and eminence in the Middle Ages in the magnificent church of St. Sernin, begun at the end of the eleventh century, which is the largest and most perfect Romanesque building in France.   The best view of the exterior is from behind the choir, where the semicircle of apsidal chapels leads the eye up to the crossing, which is crowned by a beautiful octagonal tower.   The interior, which is a replica of and contemporary with St. James of Compostella, is extremely spacious, but dark and severe, although it has the distinction of having remained unaltered since 1271.   In the ambulatory, on the inner wall, is a remarkable bas-relief of a beardless Christ in the Byzantine manner.   Less important from the æsthetic, if not from the religious, point of view is the delightful eighteenth-century tomb containing the remains of St. Sernin himself.   This is supported by stolid bulls, which serve to remind the visitor that the saint suffered martyrdom by being tied to the tail of a wild bull.   The crypt, which is mainly gothic in structure, is overcrowded with astonishing reliquaries which are of little value from either the artistic or religious point of view.

After St. Sernin, Toulouse is chiefly notable for its fine red-brick *hôtels*, which are mainly Renaissance in period.   Of these the most outstanding and ornate are the Hôtel Bernuy in the François 1er style, and the Hôtel d'Assézat, perhaps the finest house in the city, which boasts an Henri II *corps de logis* with a more austere upper storey superimposed in the middle of the seventeenth century. There is also naturally a large cathedral and a vast and bewildering museum of painting and sculpture. Details of these can be found in any guidebook, which will also remind its readers that the city is situated "on a wide curve of the Garonne where the river leaves the Pyrenean foothills and turns north-west towards the ocean."

To the east of the ancient county of Foix lies Roussillon, which to-day occupies the area of the modern department of the Pyrénées Orientales. Although Roussillon, which is so named from the red colour of its earth, has belonged to France for nearly three hundred years, in race, language, and customs its inhabitants are entirely Catalan. As in the Basque provinces on the west, the Pyrenees have also on the east made between a homogeneous people a mountain boundary which, for national convenience, eventually assumed a stable political form. During the Middle Ages Roussillon belonged to the Kings of Aragon, but in 1610 the whole of Catalonia on the north side of the Pyrenees revolted against Philip IV of Spain, and, after nearly half a century of intermittent warfare, the Treaty of the Pyrenees was signed between France and Spain by which the latter ceded the whole of Roussillon and half the Cerdagne, a small territorial division on the frontier. The portion of the Cerdagne which Spain retained is called Llivia, and is to this day completely isolated in the midst of French territory, much to the general inconvenience, owing to the hordes of customs officials necessary to protect its frontiers. French Cerdagne is the broadest valley in the Pyrenees, and is surrounded by a wall of high mountains. It is a prosperous agricultural region dotted with small villages, of which the largest and most southerly is Bourg-Madame, on the frontier. This squalid little railway terminus received its present name in 1815 in honour of the Duchess of Angoulême.

The southern part of Roussillon is dominated by the great lonely mountain of the Canigou, which gives a false impression of isolation from the main range, while its thirty-mile radius is covered with dense forests. At the foot of the Canigou lies Vernet-les-Bains, which skilfully combines a picturesque village and château with admirable anti-rheumatic waters. Lord Roberts and Mr. Rudyard Kipling were frequent visitors to this fashionable spa. To the west, Amélie-les-Bains boasts springs efficacious for skin diseases; it has been well known since Madame de Maintenon and the Duc de Maine took advantage of their curative properties in 1677. The spa received its present name in honour of Queen Marie-Amélie, the wife of Louis-Philippe, who came there for a cure in 1840.

The north-westerly approach through Roussillon to Perpignan is by

17

a grim and narrow gorge called the Défilé de Pierre-Lys. The descent is then made through the pleasant valley of the Boulzane, with its soft distant views of vineyards, cypresses, and olive-trees. Here are grown the grapes for the strong red wine of Banyuls and the white Grenache of Rivesaltes, while further south a coarser grape is made into the much advertised Byrrh. After Maury, the country begins to lose its Pyrenean aspect, and Estagel on the Agly combines the characteristics of a village in the Pyrenees with one on the Côte d'Azur. The bleak valley of the Agly, terraced with vines, debouches into a flat, featureless plain where lies Perpignan, the capital of Roussillon.

Perpignan is one of the most delightful towns in the south of France, with shady avenues, busy antique thoroughfares, and a carefree Spanish population. The most charming and original feature of the city is the Promenade des Platanes, planted in 1809, which follows a tributary of the river Tet, cutting through the centre of the town. Here in the evenings the inhabitants of Perpignan walk up and down in an animated procession, identical with the Spanish *paseo*, the sexes being usually segregated into little groups, as is the custom in Spain. At one end of the promenade a large circular café, called the *Palmarium*, resembling a mid-Victorian conservatory, collects the more idle and bibulous citizens.

The æsthetic pleasures of Perpignan are considerable but not overwhelming. The exterior of the gothic cathedral of St. Jean, begun in 1324, is ornamented with the curious herring-bone design formed by a pattern of stones in the brick walls. The interior is undistinguished except for the great width of its aisleless nave and the finely sculptured composition of the high altar, by Soler of Barcelona, which is a masterpiece of Spanish seventeenth-century ecclesiastical art. More imposing from the exterior, perhaps, is the fourteenth-century Castillet, once part of the enceinte, which is built in brick of a delicate pink. Its amorphous shape is pierced on one side by the more elegant and later Porte de Notre Dame. The museum, which is comparatively well arranged, contains the usual second-class pictures of well-known French artists, though an amusing portrait of the Duke of Orléans by Ingres and a fine Zurbaran of St. Francis rescue the collection from complete mediocrity. The gothic Loge de Mer, which is the last object of interest which the visitor need trouble to see, was built in 1397, to house the Bourse. *Loge* is derived from the Spanish *lonja*, meaning "exchange," and this gay erection is now inconsequently used as a café.

Many pleasant days can be spent in Perpignan, enjoying its simple but varied amenities, although the hotels are conducted in the Spanish

114 (*opposite*)
The Road across the Pass, Le Canigou, Roussillon

rather than in the French manner. Agreeable expeditions can also be made in the neighbourhood. There is the church at Prades to see, with its gorgeous Catalan altar-piece, and Cerbère to visit, where the Pyrenees are engulfed in the sea. The romantic ruins of the eleventh-century priory of Serrabonna are also worthy of a visit, but more important than all are the magnificent church and cloisters of Elne.

Known in pagan days as Illiberis, the town was renamed Castrum Helenæ by the Emperor Constantine in the fourth century in honour of his mother, the Empress Helena. In later times "Helenæ" was corrupted into "Elne." The Cathedral of St. Eulalia in the upper part of the town is a beautiful fortified church, built in the eleventh century and crowned with two strangely contrasting towers, one in the austere Romanesque style and the other in the more fanciful manner of the fifteenth century. The church is planned with a nave and aisles, but with no transepts, while huge piers support the round-headed arches and the vault. The lack of ornamentation and consequent simplicity of the interior are most impressive. The Romanesque cloister, situated on a terrace higher than the cathedral, is considered the finest of its period in France. The low roof is supported by an arcade of twin columns of white marble mellowed into a golden hue, while the exquisitely carved capitals depict scenes from the Old and New Testaments in the most realistic manner. The majority of these date from the twelfth and a few from the fourteenth century, and their delicate line is occasionally broken by solid quadrangular pillars.

Elne itself is an under-populated and moribund town, but on February 12th, the feast-day of St. Eulalia and St. Julia, its streets are thronged with exuberant Catalans intent on honouring their virgin patrons in their austere and crenellated cathedral.

115 (*opposite*)
Gavarnie: among the Peaks of the Pyrenees

CHAPTER IX

THE MEDITERRANEAN SEABOARD AND THE FRENCH ALPS

FROM the mist and fogs of an English February, the Mediterranean coast of France appears in the mind's eye like the Promised Land, a region of brilliant flowers, blazing sunshine, and turquoise sea; one is readily persuaded by the most unlikely posters that the impossible can happen, that a journey of a few hundred miles southward from London will transport one from cold and darkness into an exotic country of warmth and delight. It is this unquestioned optimism which often leads to disappointment, and it is as well to realise before starting that mimosa will blossom in a snowstorm and that a battle of flowers can take place in weather which would not disgrace an English March. For this reason the rare brilliant days are doubly welcome, when in the fertile little valleys of Provence, protected from the bitter wind by pinewoods on the rocky hills, almond-trees blossom in the vineyards and buds miraculously appear on the apparently moribund stumps of the vines. One such day will—and, indeed, often has to—compensate for a week of stormy weather.

The journey to the south is always intensely exciting. To leave the Gare de Lyons at night and to raise the blind of one's sleeper, if one has been fortunate enough to sleep so long, near Avignon is an experience which can be endlessly repeated without losing its dramatic effect. Fresh from the English countryside and the bleak plains of northern France, it is an unforgettable experience to look out suddenly on to the fertile valley of the Rhône, dotted with white farmhouses and dark walls of cypress, outlined against the deep red earth.

The main lines from Paris provide the most usual entry to the southern plain, which stretches below the vast twin bastions which cover half France, the French Alps, and the *Massif Central*, but there is another which is perhaps even more sensational, since a complete change comes within a few miles. Driving from the north-west, the road crosses the wide uplands of the Cevennes, as bleak and stony as the Plain of Castille, and reaches the top of the southern slope at La Caylar, whence it descends gently into the plains of Hérault. Within a mile or two the rocky wilderness gives way to typical country of the

Midi (that southern district of France which slopes towards the midday sun), a country of silver olive-trees, terraces of vines, roads bordered by thick avenues of planes, and little rivers tumbling briskly amongst smooth grey stones towards the sea.

This stretch of country, which lies between the foothills of the Cevennes and the waters of the Mediterranean, runs in a long sweep from the Pyrenees in the south to Marseilles in the east, and disappears to the north in a tall triangle up the valley of the Rhône ; it concentrates within its boundaries some of the most interesting places in France. Orographical maps colour the whole of this area a lush emerald green, and it might well be supposed that it is merely a tract of uniformly fertile country watered by the Rhône and the many other rivers which pass through it to the sea. The contrary, however, is the truth: no country could show greater variety of soil, ranging from the areas of extreme fertility south of Avignon to the stony wastes round Narbonne and the deserted salt marshes along the seaboard, where the coastline is gradually extending as the water recedes from the shallow shores. The change in geographical outlines comes with the greatest rapidity where the Rhône descends to the sea, carrying soil on the vast volume of its waters; salt lakes are formed behind this deposited soil and, in course of years, dry out into marshes, which centuries later are drained into usable land. In the time of the Roman occupation the southern half of the department of Bouches du Rhône, stretching from Arles to the sea, was a vast lake; it has taken 2,000 years for nature to convert this area into hundreds of square miles of salt marsh, and now only the industry of man can convert it into productive land.

A bountiful nature continues to make these unwelcome gifts of new country all along this stretch of coast, with the inevitable result that such towns as Narbonne, Agde, and Aigues-Mortes, once prosperous sea ports, now find themselves abandoned by the element which gave them birth and stranded like boats on a sandbank at low tide. Narbonne has found other means to industry and prosperity, but Agde and Aigues-Mortes have been compelled to give themselves up to a graceful and romantic decay.

These sunny and accessible shores have attracted succeeding nations from all parts of the Mediterranean basin. The Phœnicians made a colony here at a very early date, and were succeeded about 600 B.C. by traders from Phocæa, who founded, with the encouragement, it is said, of the Oracles of Delphi and Dodona, the colony of Massalia on a steep western hillside sloping down to an almost landlocked harbour. On this well-chosen site now stands the second city of France, Marseilles. The native Ligurians gave these cultured colonists little peace,

and they were compelled to seek the help of the Romans, who in
125 B.C. made their first entry into the country, which became known
as the *Provincia Romana* and on which they were, in the course of a
few centuries, to make an indelible mark.   Seventy-five years later the
conquest of Gaul was completed by Cæsar, and the town of Aix (*Aquæ
Sextiæ*) was founded as a capital to this important colony.

The Roman domination continued until the fifth century, when the
successful attacks of the Visigoths inaugurated centuries of turmoil
which were to pour a stream of blood on to the soil of Provence.
Under Charlemagne and Louis the Pious Provence was united to the
empire, and during the tenth century it belonged to the Kingdom of
Burgundy, following a brief period when it was in the savage hands of
the Saracens; but for the greater part of its history it had maintained its
precarious independence under the Counts of Provence, or Counts of
Arles as they were sometimes called.   A complicated descent brought
Provence in 1474 to Charles Count of Maine, nephew of Réné Duke of
Lorraine, whose successor, also Charles, left it in his will to Louis XI,
King of France.   Thus from the end of the fifteenth century it was
united with the French crown, save for a brief period in 1536 when the
Emperor Charles V, leading a successful expedition against Provence,
was crowned at Aix as King of Arles, a transitory honour which he was
unable to sustain.

The ancient title of Count of Provence was revived for Louis XVI's
plump brother, who was known by this name until he ascended the
throne as Louis XVIII in 1814.

The true extent of Provence was not very large: it stretched from
the mouth of the Rhône to the original eastern frontier of France and
northwards into the foothills of the Alps, but the name is now loosely
used to include the greater part of the Mediterranean coast and a large
part of the hinterland which was originally in the vast province of
Languedoc.   Thus the Rhône, instead of bounding Provence, which it
did until the abolition of the ancient provinces by Napoleon, now finds
itself roughly bisecting it.

A hundred miles from the sea, the valley of the Rhône opens out into
a wide triangular plain broken by scattered foothills, covered with cork
and scrubby oak-trees, amongst which are to be found many romantic
little towns.   On the west, for example, on the rising hills above
Nîmes, stands Uzés, a robust little fortified town of many towers, both
defensive and ecclesiastic;   on the ramparts, from which there is a
wide view southwards over the valley of the Gard, is the little classical
pavilion where Racine passed the year of 1661 writing one of his
earliest tragedies, *La Thébaïde*.   At the highest point of the town stands

116, 117 The Olive
Trees of Provence

118 The Walls of Aigues-Mortes

119 The Castle of Tarascon reflected in the Rhône

the Duché, the castle of the Ducs d'Uzés, the premier dukes of France, its massive mediæval walls and towers presenting a formidable exterior to the streets. In the interior courtyard, however, there is one of the prettiest little classical façades to be found in France; it is attributed to Philibert de l'Orme, but not apparently on any grounds beyond that of style.

Thirty miles away, on the eastern verges of the valley, are towns such as Capentras, with its vast seventeenth-century episcopal palace, and Vaucluse, where Petrarch composed his sonnets to Laura de Noves as he sat by the source of the Sorgue, the remarkable river which springs fully fledged as a great stream from below towering limestone cliffs. A little further east there is Gordes, a very modest replica of Uzés but also boasting a castle, though very ruined, a tremendous view of the Montagnes du Léberon, and, again like its prototype, a little restaurant where in the company of the local workers one can eat an unexpectedly excellent lunch.

Southwards, as the valley opens further, are gathered some of the most famous towns in France: Orange leads down to Avignon, Nîmes, Arles, Tarascon, and, most lovely of all, Aix-en-Provence, a crowded galaxy of stars of the architectural firmament which even Italy cannot altogether excel. Such stars they are, indeed, that their beauty and interest would be insulted by a cursory description, and it must be left to the guidebooks to furnish the necessary information.

A few miles south of Avignon the river Durance ends an adventurous career of two hundred miles or so from the mountainous frontier of Italy and loses itself in the brown waters of the Rhône; the district in the neighbourhood of their confluence is one of great fertility, and is known, at least locally, as the "Garden of Provence." To reach it, a perilous journey has to be made across one of the suspension bridges which are rather a feature of the Midi. One of the longest connects Beaucaire with Tarascon, stretching from the foot of the great castle which was completed by King Réné in the fifteenth century to the end of the important canal which connects the Rhône to the Étang du Thau near Sète. As a car or lorry crosses, the cables sway, stretch, and groan, while the roadway undulates ominously beneath its burden; but in spite of an appearance of fragility, these bridges have seldom if ever been known to deposit their charges in the waters below.

The soil in these parts is exceptionally rich, there is water in plenty, and the sun has almost as much warmth as anywhere in Europe; but there is one enemy, the wind. A biting blast tears down the valley of the Rhône and along the coast in the form of the well-known mistral; it has, indeed, the good effect of dissipating the clouds, but its cutting edge can sear young growth and distort mature trees like sea gales.   To counteract this unwelcome manifestation, the inhabitants plant thick barricades of cypress, the dark points of which form such a feature of the morning landscape when seen from the train on the way to the South.   These impenetrable hedges, often reinforced by hurdles as they lose their lower boughs, enclose little areas of rich earth, deposited many centuries ago by the Rhône and covering perhaps an acre or two, in which the early vegetables are cultivated in neat, well-kept rows. Peas, beans, tomatoes, artichokes, turnips, aubergines are sent from the neighbourhood of Avignon to the markets of northern Europe; indeed, almost the only spring vegetable not grown here is asparagus, which, however, thrives in the district of Cavaillon, some miles further east up the valley of the Durance.   Near to St. Remy vegetables give way to flowers, which, being grown for seed, are allowed to flower to their hearts' content; bright strips of ranunculus, asters, petunias are made doubly brilliant by the setting of sombre cypress.

On the southern verge of this vast kitchen garden the country opens out into the most lovely landscape in Provence.   Gentle slopes of olive fields and vineyards rise to the jagged outlines of Les Alpilles, a thin range of stony hills which juts far out into the plain.   Close to the foot of these hills a group of dark-green pine-trees almost conceals the former Priory of St. Paul, where Van Gogh spent several demented but comparatively happy years.   It was well chosen as a refuge, since it would be difficult to find any place where quiet beauty could be more soothing to a distracted mind.   Ten feet under the red earth lie the foundations of the Roman city of Glanum.   The full extent of the town has never yet been explored, but it seems probable that the Romans, with their fine sense for a site, had here a considerable colony. Two splendid Roman buildings, perhaps the finest in France, survive to show the importance of the place: a triumphal arch and a beautiful monument usually called the Mausoleum.   The former is said to have been erected by Julius Cæsar to commemorate the surrender of Vercingetorix about the year 50 B.C., and if this is correct, it is the earliest triumphal arch outside Italy;   while the Mausoleum may be said with some uncertainty to commemorate the victory of Caius Marius over the Teutons and Ambrons.   The scale of both buildings is comparatively small, and the carving of the figures has a fineness and delicacy which make it tolerably certain that they are the work of Greek craftsmen—slaves, probably, of the Romans;   they are far superior in quality to the robust and straightforward arenas in the neighbouring towns.

On a high isolated promontory which springs from the southern

120, 121   The Deserted City of Provence:
Les Baux

122 The Roman Mausoleum at St. Remy

123 Roman Remains, Vaucluse

edges of these hills stands the deserted town of Les Baux, now so ruined and decayed that it seems to be reverting into the rocks out of which it was built. During the early part of the Middle Ages it was the strongest town in the country and the chief residence of the Counts of Provence, the family which also bore at various times the tremendous titles of Princes of Orange, Kings of Arles, and Emperors of Constantinople. They were a fierce people whose characteristics have been well described by John Addington Symonds. "The stern and barren rock from which they sprang and the comet of their scutcheon are the true symbol of their natures. History records no end to their ravages and slaughters. It is a tedious catalogue of blood. . . ."

There is little evidence in this mouldering heap of structural bones, beyond an occasional early Renaissance doorway or window, to suggest that there were ever any buildings of architectural merit in Les Baux, but the ruined houses and grass-grown, deserted streets give rise to sentiments of the most pleasurable melancholy which may be allowed to reach their zenith in the little restored church, near the summit of the hill, where, in the dark and dripping Carolingian chapel hewn from the live rock, so much history has passed. The decay of this magnificent fortress began when it passed to Charles of Anjou in the thirteenth century, while demolition of the castle and fortifications, which was begun by Louis XI, was completed during the first half of the seventeenth century by Louis XIII. Thus the town, which once housed thousands, now contains less than a hundred inhabitants; indeed, it seems remarkable that there should still be so many, since until a few years ago there was neither light nor water on this rocky pinnacle. In summer the sun, beating down on the treeless ruins, turns the town into a furnace; while in the winter the wind blows so fiercely down the valley that it is impossible to stand against it. Those who choose to pass their lives in Les Baux must be tough and obdurate characters.

On the southern side of the town a sheer precipice of several hundred feet drops to a green plain which stretches away in an unbroken expanse until, on the far horizon, the green imperceptibly melts into the pale blue of the distant Mediterranean. Across this green plain wind the two great branches of the Rhône, between which lies the deserted Île de la Camargue, a stony, swampy area gradually developing from a salt lake into dry, if not fertile, land. Here and there a few plots of ground on slightly higher levels have been cleared and planted with vines; but it is not so far an enterprise which has met with sufficient success to encourage any extensive effort at reclamation. In general, the sour

18

soil is abandoned to its natural covering of coarse scrub, amongst which roam the wild bulls used at the fights in the arenas of Provence.

On the southern shore of the Camargue, lying close to the mouth of the western branch of the river, the Petit Rhône, is the village of Les Stes. Maries-de-la-Mer, the legendary site of the landing of the little company of Christian exiles who were driven from Judæa after the Crucifixion. The party consisted of Mary Jacob, sister of the Virgin, Mary Salome, mother of James and John, Sarah, their coloured servant, with Mary Magdalen, Martha, Lazarus, and Maximin. Mary Jacob, Mary Salome, and Sarah lived the remainder of their lives on the shore to which they had been so miraculously wafted, and their bodies now lie in the sturdy thirteenth-century church, which, like the finer example at Agde further west, is as much a fortress as a religious building. The massive, almost windowless walls, built up in large blocks of lava stone, are crowned by machicolations and battlements above which rises a formidable tower.

In the crypt lies the body of Sarah, an object of the greatest veneration to the gipsies, who come many hundreds of miles during the month of May to attend the festival of their patron; while in a room formed in the tower and lined with exceedingly mundane eighteenth-century *boiseries* are the bodies of Mary Jacob and Mary Salome, encased in elaborate wooden coffins. On their feast-days these heavy chests are lowered with considerable difficulty by an elaborate system of wind-lasses and flower-covered ropes from this pretty Louis XV salon into the church below.

A harder fate was reserved for Mary Magdalen, who, wishing to expiate her sins by passing the remaining years of her life in the solitude of a hermit, left her companions and wandered eastwards across the plains south of Arles. She came at last to a high range of hills, now known as the Chaine de la Ste. Baume, in the deserted heart of the *Provincia Romana*; high up in the precipitous northern face she dis-covered a large cave in which rose a spring of pure water, and in the cold and damp of this rocky isolation she passed the remainder of her days. Death, however, was not the end of her adventures. Her body, with the exception of an arm which still remains in the cave, was transported, by divine agency it is said, to the church founded by St. Maximin in the plain far below. Here it was suitably housed in suc-ceeding buildings, remaining until 1789 in the church, which is the finest of the rare gothic buildings in Provence. In the wave of iconoclasm which accompanied the Revolution the saint's body was burnt, but her head was somehow preserved, and can now be seen in the crypt set in a realistic ormolu bust dating from the middle of the last century. The brown skull gazing from the gaudy frame of luxuriant golden curls is a relic which can be guaranteed to produce the most chastening emotions in every wayward character.

The saint's cave in the hills has now been formed into a chapel, and a path worn through centuries by the feet of the pious has made the ascent to it practicable though arduous. In this arid pine-growing district it is remarkable to find the lower slopes of the range covered with a thick forest of deciduous trees; beech, oak, and ash thrive on this northern slope, which the Magdalen's spring keeps as wet and mossy as an English wood.

From the terrace before the cave, a distant view across barren hills and pine-covered valleys is bounded by the stony barricade of the Montagne Ste. Victoire, the angular outline of which has become familiar from the pictures of Cézanne. On the plain below was fought, in 102 B.C., the fiercest battle of the Roman campaigns, in which Marius defeated and destroyed a host of barbarians; a hundred thousand men are said to have perished in the fight, and the stream of the Arc was choked with their bodies.

Twenty miles west of Les Stes. Maries-de-la-Mer, beyond a desperate waste of swamps, rise the tremendous walls of Aigues-Mortes, reached by a causeway raised above the level of the surrounding marsh. It is the most famous of several towns on this coast which have been deserted by the Mediterranean, but although the receding sea has ruined the town commercially, it has done it an invaluable service architecturally. Instead of being lost amongst the inevitable building accretions of prosperity, the fortifications still rise almost as isolated as when they were built, and the declining population is easily contained within the walls. There was a small Roman settlement on the site of the present town, a fishing-village or perhaps a modest port, but St. Louis (1215–1270) was the first to turn it into a place of consequence. He built the Tour de Constance, the splendid circular keep, with walls five yards thick, which stands at the north-west corner; he also dredged the lagoon so that it might have sufficient depth for the passage of his fleet when leaving for the Crusades. From Aigues-Mortes St. Louis embarked for Egypt in 1248 and again in 1270, in the pious attempt to convert the King of Tunis to Christianity, an expedition which ended in his death from plague at Carthage. The saint's son, Philip the Bold (1245–1285), constructed the vast rectangle of battlemented walls, strengthened by fifteen towers and pierced by ten gates, which, after sympathetic restoration, still stand as splendidly as when they were built. The sea has now far receded, but from the battlements a distant line of blue can be seen across marshes studded with the white pyramids of salt which provide the one remaining industry of the town.

Inland from the lagoons of this flat, indented coast the country adopts a contrasting aspect of luxuriance; the gently undulating landscape is planted thickly with vines, which, broken by occasional groups of trees, stretch away as far as the eye can reach. The quantity of wine produced by these vineyards is prodigious, but the quality is not very high, though it is agreeable enough when drunk in the district.

The centre of the wine trade is Montpellier, the capital of the department of Hérault, a charming town of wide streets and spacious squares. In the middle of the eighteenth century the necessity for a water supply led to the construction of a magnificent aqueduct of two tiers of graceful arches, which, bringing water from the neighbouring hills, strides into the town on the west side and pours its burden into a beautiful pavilion known as the Château d'Eau. This pillared temple, which rises from a stone-rimmed pool, is remarkable for the delicacy of its ornamentation, in which fish-nets appropriately take the place of the conventional wreaths and swags. It forms the central feature of a fine formal garden laid out by d'Aviler, in which pleached lime-trees, gravel walks, and stone balustrades lead up to the Porte du Peyron, a triumphal arch erected towards the end of the eighteenth century in memory of Louis XIV.

Montpellier has a distinction, almost unique among French towns, of having given its name to squares and streets in London, Cheltenham, and Brighton. This rare compliment appears to be due to the popularity of the town during the eighteenth century with the many English visitors who went there to take the waters and breath the salubrious air.

The sweep of country running southward from Montpellier between the mountains and the sea contains several towns of commercial importance and also of considerable interest, although in a district where the architectural standard is so high they can hardly be placed in the front rank. Sète, or Cette, for example, perched on a stony slope between the Étang de Thau and the sea, is not architecturally distinguished, but the maze of wide canals which pass through the lower part of the town is extremely picturesque. And Béziers also has considerable character once the spreading commercial suburbs have been penetrated ; the steep and narrow streets of the old town lead to the formidable battlemented church of St. Nazaire, the epitome of the church militant, which, from a high bastion on the summit of a conical hill, frowns menacingly towards the distant foothills of the Pyrenees.

The third town of this district, Narbonne, is considerably more attractive than its neighbours. The site, originally on the banks of a

124   Toulon: Summer Evening on the Quai Kronstadt

125   Avignon : Spahis marching past the Palace of the Popes

126　The Old Port of Marseilles

127　Marseilles: a Street of the Old Port

128 Grenoble: a Stepped Street of the
Old Quarter

129 The Côte d'Azur at St. Tropez

130   A Village in the Dauphiné, near Le Lautaret

131   A Gorge in the Isère

deep indentation of the sea, made it an ideal harbour for the Romans, and for many centuries it rivalled Marseilles in importance and gave its name to a large province. But gradually the harbour shallowed into a lagoon and the lagoon into a marsh, until the town now finds itself as much as five miles from the sea and dependent for maritime trade on the Canal de la Robine, which, passing through the lagoons, reaches the Mediterranean at the little harbour of La Nouvelle.

The canal, as it intersects the town, is the centre of commercial and social life. The barges on its waters may come from the Mediterranean or they may have made the long journey across France from the distant Atlantic by means of the Canal du Midi. The plane-shaded promenades along the banks form the principal walk for the inhabitants, and on summer evenings the Narbonnais in hundreds sit or stroll amongst the trees, whose trunks gleam like white pillars supporting the dark green canopy above.

On a hill above the canals stands the astonishing cathedral of St. Just. It was begun in 1272, in tall gothic style and on a majestic scale, but funds were exhausted by the time the chancel was completed, and it is cut short abruptly at the point where the transepts should have branched out. It was unlikely that the rich years of the eighteenth century should have passed without an attempt being made to complete the work, and towards the middle of it an enterprising bishop began to build a nave on a scale suitable to the existing chancel, but in a remarkable bastard style which can only be supposed to have been the product of his own fertile invention; it is neither Romanesque, nor gothic, nor classical, although it includes features from all three styles, and it is impossible to envisage what its appearance would have been had it ever been completed—for the Cathedral of Narbonne was destined to remain a fragment, and the golden stone walls, shafts, and buttresses of the bishop's incompleted fantasy now stand as a melancholy addition to this strange building.

The town is encircled on the south and west by country as barren as any in Europe; the low, rocky hills support nothing beyond a sparse covering of herbs, such as rosemary, mint, and thyme, which find a meagre sustenance among the sun-baked stones. Within a few miles, however, nature becomes less stubborn, and, although the hills remain sterile, the valleys between bear a precarious crop of grapes, while here and there appear groups of trees encouraged by some little stream.

In one of these watered and wooded valleys lies the Abbey of Fontfroide, a splendid Benedictine monastery dating from the twelfth and thirteenth centuries, but now in private ownership. The buildings are complete and have been sympathetically restored; there are a vast

Transitional church and great stone-vaulted passages and halls, which must form a rather ghostly adjunct to a private house, but the gem is the Romanesque cloister, an outstanding example even in this country which is so rich in Romanesque architecture.

Further westward along the valley of the Aude, where the stony hills give way to a pastoral and well-wooded countryside, lies the Mecca of the late-Victorian tourist, Carcassonne. The first sight of the Cité is, indeed, magnificent: grey walls, battlements, and gateways, fifty towers running to conical roofs, and a superbly romantic outline which gives the town a fabulous and fairy-story appearance. But closer inspection reveals all too clearly the drastic work of the ubiquitous Viollet-le-Duc (1814–1879), who by his intensive restoration and rebuilding transformed a romantic ruin into a hard, neat, and absolutely soulless replica of a mediæval fortified town.

The Mediterranean coast of France can be divided into two distinct divisions, which correspond roughly to the provinces of Languedoc and Provence, the former flat and shallow, the latter high and indented, with steep, rocky cliffs crowned with pinewoods. The most beautiful part of the coast is the stretch from Marseilles to St. Tropez, which has Toulon harbour at its most southerly point, and has none of the cosmopolitan magnificence of the more popular part of the Côte d'Azur further east. Marseilles strikes the note for the whole district. In spite of its varied population, no town is more essentially French, none combines so strikingly the air of bourgeois life and prosperity, as typified in the Cannebière, its central street, with the feeling of almost Oriental mystery which pervades the narrow streets round the Old Port. In this mixture of contrasting characteristics the charm of the town lies rather than in any architectural merits, though there is considerable beauty in the great horseshoe of sunny quays which branches from the bottom of the Cannebière round the Inner Harbour. The few buildings of merit are contained in the labyrinth of dark streets to the north of the harbour, but an earnest student of architecture, who may wish to study the baroque façade of the seventeenth-century town hall, will find his quiet contemplation considerably harassed by the harpies of the neighbourhood, who, with a technique all their own, will remove hat, handkerchief, and even spectacles before he has recovered from his astonishment at the attack.

Across a wide range of broken, pine-covered hills lies Toulon, the most important naval station in the country. The upper part of the town near the main road is modern, and it is thus easy to pass through without discovering the beauty and charm of the old streets and quays adjoining the waterfront. The Quai Kronstadt is lined with restaurants and cafés in which it is enchanting to spend an hour on a hot summer night. In front spread the dark waters of the Inner Harbour backed by the many-coloured lights of ships; behind rise tall, reserved façades in stone and stucco, some, such as the old Hôtel de Ville, ornamented with baroque carving by Puget; between lies the Quai, its grey stones teeming with an infinitely varied collection of passers-by, ranging from a sprinkling of exotics from the neighbouring joytowns to flocks of sailors in their white summer uniforms.

Around the great bay of Toulon lie some of the prettiest and most sequestered parts of the coast. Here and there little dusty roads plunge southwards amongst the pine-covered hills to the sea or end abruptly on the cliff's edge; but there are long stretches of rocky shore which can only be reached on foot down some precipitous path. To the east of the bay the steep hillsides have in many places been cleared of their natural covering of trees and evergreen shrubs and formed into narrow terraces on which flowers are cultivated for the spring markets. From morning till night the peasants and their children work amongst the beds of narcissi, stocks, anemones, and irises. Crowning the hills, far above the terraces and concealed amongst the pines and arbutus, are great forts built for the protection of Toulon harbour, while below the blue sea breaks on the rocks of deserted shores. All about the terraces the spring wildflowers, asphodel, valerian, pink gladioli, bushes of cistus and broom, make almost as fine a show as those which are cultivated; the variety may not be as great, but the effect is prodigious.

Flowers are not the only product of these remote hills; high on a steep slope is a copper-mine which was owned by Bolo Pasha, who was executed during the war as a spy. The deserted sheds, the refinery, and the piles of viridian stone now stand as perhaps his only memorial.

From the wide vine-covered plain which lies inland from the coast narrow valleys run northwards into the hills; they are green and fertile with the waters of streams, and are famous for their cherries, which are the earliest in the country. Mounting to the north of the department of Var, the hills become wild and stony, giving a foretaste of the Alps which lie beyond, but in spite of its rude aspect the district produces two most elegant crops, lavender and truffles. The former thrives on the stony fields at an elevation of two or three thousand feet, but the latter is a more tender organism, and requires a curious form of cultivation. The scrubby oaks which cover the hills and grow to little more than fifteen feet in height are thinned into widely separated lines, and the stony ground within a yard of their roots is cleared of all vegetation. The cultivator then sits down to wait, since no means is known of starting the growth of truffles, and it is not until he locates the hoped-for fungus with the aid of his pig that he knows if his labours have been rewarded.

Northwards, as the hills rise towards the Alps, the towns become fewer and less interesting; in general they crouch deep down in river valleys, as, for example, the picturesque town of Castellane on the Verdon and Manosque in the wider valley of the Durance. Sisteron, however, further north, is built in a strategic position where the river narrows into a gorge below the unassailable hill on which stands the citadel.

North of Sisteron, the Durance forms the boundary between the departments of Basses-Alpes and Hautes-Alpes, and so between Provence and the mountainous province of Dauphiné, which stretches from the left bank of the Rhône to the frontier of Italy. This change of province marks also a distinct alteration of the landscape, an alteration both of quality and of scale. Outlines become larger and wilder, and there is no longer that feeling, as in Provence, that however barren the immediate prospect, there are sunny, fertile slopes just out of sight.

The name of Dauphiné indicates a close connection with the Royal House of France, which, in fact, it has had since the fourteenth century. During its very early history it maintained a difficult independence under rulers who bore the title of Count or Dauphin of the Viennois; the last of these, Humbert II, sold his dominions in 1349, the year of his death, to Charles of Valois, who on his succession to the throne of France as Charles V gave Dauphiné to his eldest son, since which time the title was always borne by the king's heir.

The country of Dauphiné has not the attraction for the tourist of Savoy, which lies to the north. The towns are sparsely scattered amongst the hills and are, on the whole, of little architectural import- ance, while the landscape of wide deep valleys merging into great stony slopes which rise to wild rocky peaks is almost overwhelming in its scale. Swift-flowing rivers race amongst the stones, finding some escape from the sunless valleys which seem to the eye to be everywhere closed by savage mountain ranges; it is possible in this vast silent country to feel the effects of both claustro- and agoraphobia simul- taneously. But others may find a soothing influence in a country where the scale is so great that the human species seems to be of the utmost insignificance.

The roads follow by necessity close to the rivers, and of these the Durance provides the most picturesque route through this section of the Alps. In the plains of Provence this lovely river is broad, yellow, and usually gently-flowing, but amongst the mountains it has the high spirits

132 (*opposite*)
The Field Patchwork of Savoy

of youth, and tumbles, a streak of pale green, amongst the white stones of its twisting bed. The soil in these valleys is poor and scarce, in many places little more than a thin covering over the rocky substratum, but wherever there is a depth of a few inches the earth is industriously tilled by the peasants; thus all about the lower slopes are little patches, sometimes covering no more than a few square yards, given over to the cultivation of corn, vines, or vegetables. The middle slopes below the final peaks are clothed with forest, great drifts of larch and spruce thriving wherever there is sufficient earth to give them roothold.

The villages clearly indicate the hard lives of the inhabitants. The cottages are built of stone and wood, the two principal products of the country, and are huddled together in sad, untidy groups with none of the beauty or the air of prosperity of the Swiss Alpine villages. Close to the junction of the Durance and the Guil stands a rocky conical hill known as Mont Dauphin, on the summit of which Vauban erected fortifications built in a rose-pink stone quarried in the neighbouring mountain-sides.

Twenty miles further north, near the agreeable winter-sports centre of Briançon, one bids farewell to the Durance, which is such an invaluable guide through the Western Alps, and follows the Guisane into the heart of the mountains. The road mounts from the valley to the Col de Lautaret at a height of over 6,000 feet, a pass well known to the Romans, since to the east lay the way over the Oisans to Grenoble. Northwards it zigzags breathlessly up a further 2,000 feet to the Col du Galibier, the second highest pass in France and the third in Europe. The southern slopes of the mountains are famous for their spring wild-flowers, but the northern face, towards the summit of the pass, is often deep in snow throughout the year. The tunnel, which now saves the traveller a climb of several hundred extra feet, may mark a violent transition from summer to winter: leaving the brown hillsides of Dauphiné, one emerges into the snows of Savoy, with, so it seems, the whole of this lovely province at one's feet. Eastwards from Le Lautaret, the road meets the river Romanche, and descends with it to Grenoble, which lies in the wide valley of the Isère.

The capital of Dauphiné is a prosperous commercial town with all the older attributes, such as a bishopric and a university, to give it civic importance; industrially its main product is leather gloves. But the principal charm comes from its position in a deep valley of the moun-tains, so deep that the view along every street is closed by a near or distant hill or mountain peak. The old streets and squares crowd in some confusion along the left bank of the Isère, while on the further

19

L'Aiguille du Dru, a Peak of the French Alps near Chamonix

side rise steep hills crowned by the geometrical outlines of a number of forts.

Grenoble will always be remembered for its adherence to the cause of Napoleon on his return from Elba. At the little town of Laffrey, a few miles south, he was first acclaimed by the old soldiers who had been sent by the Bourbons to arrest him. The same day, March 7th, 1815, he came into Grenoble, and was received with the wildest enthusiasm, which was echoed as he moved northward. The welcome given him in Dauphiné made possible the short triumph of a hundred days which was to finish with his final defeat at Waterloo.

From the northern side of the Col du Galibier a steep, twisting road, winding amongst the trunks of giant spruce, leads down to the river Arc, the valley of which formed, during the Roman occupation, one of the main connections between Italy and western Europe. The district, which is known as the Maurienne, has the distinction of being one of the earliest acquisitions of the House of Savoy, the dynasty which, after nine centuries of rule over Savoy and Piedmont, now reigns over Italy.

The family has an interesting link with England: Victor Amadeus II (1675–1732) married Anne of Orleans, who was a daughter of Henrietta of England and a granddaughter of Charles I. Through this marriage the family could boast a claim to the English throne prior, except for the bar of religion, to that of the House of Hanover. In 1831, how-ever, the main line became extinct, and the inheritance of Sardinia, Savoy, Piedmont, and Genoa passed to a distant cousin, Charles Albert, whose son Victor Emmanuel (1849–1879) was proclaimed King of Italy on February 18th, 1861.

Following the valley of the Arc, the road passes through high barren hills until it reaches the banks of the Isère, where the scenery changes with astonishing rapidity. Mountains give way to widely spaced hills covered with hanging woods of beech and ash; in the broad valley between grow vines, maize, pumpkins, and all sorts of vegetables, while pale-brown cows graze amongst the purple drifts of crocus in the closely cut meadows. The villages have a prosperous air: the houses are large and are built in the Swiss style, with widely projecting roofs as protection against the snow, and the gardens are well kept and bright with flowers. This fertile valley affords a welcome contrast to the sad, barren hill-rifts of the Dauphiné.

Amongst the lovely green hills on the borders of Savoie and Haute-Savoie lie the only two lakes of any size in France, if one excepts Geneva: the Lac du Bourget and Lac d'Annecy, which are as beautiful on their smaller scale as the lakes of northern Italy. Le Bourget is the larger but the less famous, perhaps because it has no town actually on its shores, though both Aix-les-Bains and Chambéry are only a short distance away. The former is set back no more than a mile or so, but its vast modern hotels and thermal stations are discreetly hidden in a fold of the hills, and only the Old Port, with its stone piers, fishing-boats, and little paddle-steamers, backed by a canopy of pleached plane-trees concealing several superb restaurants, can be seen from the water. On the west side of the lake, high wooded hills descend to the water's edge, giving little opportunity for building, except for one long low promontory on which stands the romantic and intensely interesting Abbaye d'Hautcombe. This abbey was founded eight hundred years ago by St. Bernard and Count Amadeus II of Savoy. The main buildings were rebuilt in the eighteenth-century in a dignified classical style, but the church, which is of considerable size, was reconstructed by Charles-Felix, King of Sardinia and Count of Savoy, between the years 1824 and 1843. The Cathedral of Milan served as a model, and led to a wild orgy of decorated gothic, in which the heaviest and most elaborate ornamentation was introduced regardless of the difference in scale between church and cathedral. There are many interesting monuments to the family of Savoy, the most charming being a life-sized statue of Charles-Felix's wife, Marie-Christine of Naples, portrayed in the romantic fashions of 1830, though it was not in fact executed by Albertoni until a quarter of a century later. The queen passed the greater part of her widowhood in the abbey, and her simple rooms still preserve their modest 1820 furniture, striped wallpapers and draped hangings surrounding long windows looking southward down the length of the lake. These rooms, but no other part of the abbey, are the private property of the King of Italy, who is descended from Charles-Felix's cousin and successor.

A few miles from beyond Chambéry, on a southern slope of the hill, stands Les Charmettes, the house in which Jean-Jacques Rousseau came to live with Madame de Warens towards the end of the summer of 1736. The rooms are few but spacious, and their panelled and painted walls have an air of elegance which one would not expect from the bucolic exterior; the immediate surroundings, with tousled garden and little vineyard leading to the chestnut woods, may well be as they were two centuries ago.

Between the Lac du Bourget and the Lac d'Annecy lies a lovely undulating country of radiant, fertile valleys, in which are grown maize and vegetables as well as the vines which produce the rather sour wine of the country, such as Crépy; but the greater part of the slopes is given up to meadows, which yield several crops of grass in a season and in September are mauve with autumn crocus.

The Lac d'Annecy has perhaps spectacular advantages over its neighbours. It is as Como compared to Garda, with the former's broken outline of high, dark-green hills reflected in pale, still waters and set against a panorama of majestic mountain peaks. The great valley in which it lies has a curious quality of silence, a silence almost of a deserted land.

The air of desertion is, however, an extreme delusion; although the eastern shore is comparatively sequestered, except for an occasional hotel and the charming little town of Talloires, on the western shore a chain of hotels and restaurants concealed amongst the trees leads the traveller into the town of Annecy at the head of the lake.

Few towns create such an impression of distinction and character while containing so few buildings of particular architectural merit as Annecy. This may be due to the fact that it has evolved an individual feature in its streets of robust arcades, supporting simple seventeenth-century façades, a structural style which has almost its only counterpart at La Rochelle, hundreds of miles away on the Atlantic coast. On the south side of the town stands the castle, mediæval but considerably restored, while round the foot of the precipitous rock on which it is built cluster the narrow streets and canals along which, under dark tunnels of plane-trees, one can catch a glimpse of the gleaming waters of the lake.

Northwards from Annecy the mountains and uplands of Chablais stretch away to the shores of the Lake of Geneva, which bounds the province and the country. It was upon this landscape that Gibbon looked from his house at Lausanne far across the water. "From the garden a rich scenery of meadows and vineyards descends to the Leman lake, and the prospect far beyond the lake is crowned by the stupendous mountains of Savoy."

INDEX

(The numerals in italics refer to the *figure numbers* of illustrations)

ANJOU

St. Nazaire — Loire — ANGERS — Blois — Chambord — Cheverny

TOURS — Vouvray — Chaumont — Amboise

NANTES — Saumur — Longeais — Luynes — Chinon — Azay le Rideau — Vierzon

BOURGES

Les Sables — La Roche sur Yon — POITOU — Loudun — Richelieu — Chatellerault — Valencay

Parthenay — POITIERS — Indre

Fontenay le Comte — Nouaillés — St. Savin — Montmorillon

Niort — Lusignan

La Rochelle — Melle — Charente

Rochefort — St. Pierre — I. d'Oléron — Pert. de Maumusson — Marennes — ANGOUMOIS — Limoges

Saintes — Cognac — Jarnac — ANGOULÊME

Royan — Talmont — Pons — Echebonne — Montagne — St. Fort — Jonzac

Aubeterre — Dronne — Hautefort — Corrèze

Ribérac — PERIGUEUX — BRIVE

DORDOGNE

Gironde — Libourne — St. Emilion — Bergerac — Sarlat — Beaulieu — St. Cére

BORDEAUX — Dordogne — Aur

Arcachon — Barsac — Langon — Lot — Cahors

Pte d'Arcachon — Agen

LANDES — Garonne — MONTAUBON — Cordes

Midouze — Mont de Marsan — Tarn — Albi

Dax — St. Sever — Adour — Auch — TOULOUSE — Carcassonne

Biarritz — BAYONNE — Ortnez — Sauveterre — Pau — Tarbes — St. Gaudens — Fontf

St. Jean-Pied-de-Port — Mauléon — Oloron — Lourdes — Bagnères — St. Bertrand — St. Lizier — St. Girons — Foix

Iroisville — Aramits — Campan — Arreau

Roncesvalles — Eaux Chaudes — Cauterets — St. Girons

Gabas — Gavarnie — Bagnères de Luchon

Somport — La Brèche de Roland — PERPIGN — Prad — Vernet

ANDORRA — Bourg-Madame — Canigou

SPAIN